PRAISE FOR *HOW WE READ THE BIBLE*

"Many churches spend their energy trying to 'get it right' when it comes to WHAT the Bible is and WHAT the Bible says. This is especially true when it comes to how many churches engage their young people.

"Through Matt's unique story and perspective, he invites us into a broader experience of HOW we read the Bible and challenges us to consider that there are more 'how's' than we could have imagined. This book will help people move from using the Bible only to gain information, and into a growing relationship with the Bible and a lifelong journey of transformation."

RICHARD ROHR, OFM, author of *The Divine Dance*

"This book by Matt Laidlaw is going to be used widely by youth workers who are concerned about biblical illiteracy among young people today. Matt provides outstanding directives on how to get young people involved in the Bible and how to get them discussing how the Bible relates to their everyday experiences. I give this book two thumbs up."

TONY CAMPOLO, author, speaker, and a founder of the *Red Letter Christians* movement

"Laidlaw charts a course from the shores of reading the Bible to the deep waters of allowing the Bible to lead us in youth ministry. In a journey with the author from the shores of Lake Superior to the Sea of Galilee, this resource will immerse your ministry—and more importantly your own spiritual journey—in rich biblical reflection and thoughtful practice with young people."

ABIGAIL VISCO RUSERT, Director, Institute for Youth Ministry, Princeton Theological Seminary

"This book is for the heroes who dream big about how students can form a different kind of relationship with the words of God. I'm a fan of anyone who begs us to stick with students in the questions and dissonance that result when we let the Bible shape who we are. Matt gives us engaging help to reframe the way we experience the Bible."

BROOKLYN LINDSEY, recovering youth minister, writer, speaker, church planter of Somos Church, Lakeland, Florida

"Some theorists have argued that we're living in a post-reading world. Fewer people are reading books, and even fewer are reading newspapers. YouTube and Netflix have become ubiquitous. Youth workers have a struggle ahead of them; not only do they need to convince young people to read, but to read an ancient text for meaning and direction in their lives today. While young people might think it an option not to read, the depth of the Christian tradition and the importance of discerning the action of the living God make reading the biblical text essential. Right at the crux of this tension, Matt Laidlaw offers all of us an incredibly helpful resource to find our way productively through this reality. I promise this little book will open your mind about reading the Bible and impact your young people. It is a treasure."

ANDREW ROOT, Professor of Youth and Family Ministry, Luther Seminary and author of *Exploding Stars, Dead Dinosaurs, and Zombies: Youth Ministry in an Age of Science*

"I wish Matt Laidlaw had been my pastor when I was a teenager. I wish this book had been at my disposal when I started ministry 20+ years ago. The words of this book are freeing and frustrating, filling and full, foundational and future focused. Not only did I feel challenged and provoked in my own discipleship, but I was inspired as a teacher to teenagers today. If you want to capture the imagination of teenagers with the wholeness of the Gospel, read this before you teach again."

APRIL DIAZ, aprildiaz.com

FULLER YOUTH INSTITUTE

How We Read the Bible
8 Ways to Engage the Bible with Our Students

Foreword by Kara Powell

Copyright © 2018 by Matthew J. Laidlaw
All Rights Reserved

Published in the United States of America by
Fuller Youth Institute, 135 N. Oakland Ave., Pasadena, CA, 91182
fulleryouthinstitute.org

ISBN 978-0-9914880-6-3

Cover and Interior Design: Macy Phenix Davis
Copy Editor: Joy Netanya Thompson
Senior Editor: Brad M. Griffin
Printed in the United States of America

8 WAYS TO ENGAGE THE
BIBLE WITH OUR STUDENTS

HOW
WE
READ
THE
BIBLE

MATT LAIDLAW

FOREWORD BY KARA POWELL

For Stephanie, Ezekiel, and Evelyn
May we keep going and keep growing

TABLE OF CONTENTS

FOREWORD

BY KARA POWELL

I love God's Word. And I want leaders like you and young people like the ones in your ministry to feel the same.

I keep my favorite Bible on the bottom shelf of our living room coffee table. Most mornings, in between exercising, checking email, and getting our family ready for the day, I sit in our living room for at least a few minutes and center myself in prayer and Scripture. Time in God's Word is a priority for me.

Which is why it's surprising that I've often handled Scripture so poorly in youth ministry.

Far too many Sundays to count, I figured out on my own what students needed to hear in my teaching, and then looked for a Bible verse that would affirm my main point. (In case you're wondering—yes, that's called "proof-texting.")

This is embarrassing to admit, but there was also the season in high school ministry when I joked with other youth pastors about writing a book called *How to Give a Youth Group Talk Without Using the Bible*. Who needed the Bible when we could come up with creative talk ideas on our own?

But probably my lowest point in engaging students with Scripture came during a busy season in middle school ministry. I was a full-time seminary student and part-time middle school pastor, which left me not very much time to prepare my Sunday and midweek talks. So, I turned to published worksheets that were touted as "easy to prepare." Typically, the day before I had to speak, I would work from the worksheets and craft my talk in less than ten minutes.

Once, I used those worksheets to create an entire talk in a drive-through line at a fast-food restaurant on my way to church. I placed my order, and while waiting for my fries and burger, I got out the worksheet and a pen and made a few notes. Ninety seconds later, I tossed the worksheet in the backseat, pulled forward to pick up my dinner, and headed to church.

As a reminder, *I was a seminary student while all this was happening*. I was spending twenty to thirty hours per week studying God's Word for my master's degree and it was changing my own life. But I had no idea how to help the power of those same scriptures change the lives of the teenagers I saw every week.

That's why I'm so grateful for this new Fuller Youth Institute (FYI) resource from our friend Matt Laidlaw. I needed this tool when I was a hands-on youth leader. I'm betting you do too.

It has always bothered me when teachers and leaders suggest that our job is to "make" God's Word relevant for young people. God's Word is *already* relevant to young people. Our job is to help that relevance shine forth. You

God's Word is already relevant to young people. Our job is to help that relevance shine forth.

will get better at that task thanks to Matt's fresh insights and real-life ministry examples of how he finds the intersection between students' current lives and Scripture's timeless stories.

This book is a bit different from FYI's typical resources. While it's grounded in research, it's also heavily influenced by Matt's own experience reading the Bible and teaching it to students. Your story and your context are likely different from Matt's. I know mine are. But I found many elements of Matt's narrative that converged with mine, and those that didn't have stretched me to see my story in new ways. I'm optimistic the same will happen for you.

Our team is hopeful that you will use and re-use this book over the years as it inspires you to ...

- Dream new dreams for your youth ministry teaching and small groups.

- Look for new meanings and insights in familiar Bible passages.

- Equip every volunteer, teacher, and small group leader to better connect the dots between students' questions and the Bible's responses—even if those responses pose more questions.

- Give students a vision for how they can encounter Scripture during their own personal times of reading and reflection.

- Empower parents to have better discussions with their kids about Scripture.

- Carve out time in your busy schedule to journey through Scripture—even (and maybe especially) when it's not to prepare your next talk, but rather for your own growth.

Thanks to this book, that last hope has already happened in me. I feel more inspired to carve out minutes and hours to sift through the phrases and pages of the Bible passages that I love. I'm guessing the same will happen for you. As a result, I hope your students will fall more in love with the Bible, too.

Kara Powell

Kara Powell
Executive Director, Fuller Youth Institute
Pasadena, California

INTRODUCTION

A MAP TO REIMAGINE

The L<small>ORD</small> said to Abram, "Leave your land, your family, and your father's household for the land that I will show you."

GENESIS 12:1A

"WHAT'S WRONG WITH THAT MAP?"

There is a map of the world on the wall in my 7-year-old son's bedroom.

Whenever I look at it, I feel disoriented.

When other friends or family members have seen it, they stop and look, often for an extended period of time—just staring at it until someone or something else interrupts them.

When one family member first noticed it, he asked, "What's wrong with that map?"

My wife and I grew up in families where we didn't travel far from home, and weren't raised to consider that there are other people who are different from us living in different parts of the world, or for that matter, our own state or town. Since we've been married, we've done our best to travel as much as we're able, and we want to raise our kids to have a broader world than the one with which we were raised. In some small way, the map on the wall in my son's bedroom is meant to help with this, because it's not like a map we've ever seen before.

Rather than centering the map on North America and the Atlantic Ocean, this map places the North Pole at the center. Even though it's been on the wall in my son's room for years, I still find myself staring at it. It sparks curiosity when I see the proximity of countries and oceans to one another from a different perspective than I've been conditioned to see throughout my life. I've noticed towns, mountains, and rivers that I had never heard of before. That map has actually created desire to understand parts of the world I hadn't previously desired to experience.

Which naturally leads us to the story of a Bedouin family from the Middle East 4,000 years ago. It's the story of Abram and Sarai in Genesis 12. If you're not familiar with the Bible, at this point in the story, just twelve chapters in, it's not going well. God has already banished the first humans from the Garden of Eden for their disobedience, one of the first humans murdered his brother, and later the sin of humans was so offensive to God that God destroyed the earth with a flood, sparing only one righteous family. Things didn't go great with that family, and eventually humans try to build a tower to heaven to be like God. As a corrective to their power-seeking and empire-building, God gives languages and disperses the people more broadly.

Things need to change, but rather than banishing humans from the garden, sending a flood, or destroying a tower and shooing people away, God takes a different approach:

> The LORD said to Abram, "Leave your land, your family, and your father's household for the land that I will show you. I will make of you a great nation and will bless you. I will make your name respected, and you will be a blessing.
>
> I will bless those who bless you, those who curse you I will curse; all the families of the earth will be blessed because of you."

> Abram left just as the LORD told him, and Lot went with him. Now Abram was 75 years old when he left Haran. Abram took his wife Sarai, his nephew Lot, all of their possessions, and those who became members of their household in Haran; and they set out for the land of Canaan.

GENESIS 12:1-5A

God shows up to Abram, a character we only learn a little bit about in the previous chapter, and makes a promise to him and to his wife Sarai: *I will bless you greatly, and will bless the world greatly through you.*

This is the beginning of God's rescue plan for a world spiraling out of control; the beginning of the nation of Israel, the family line of the Messiah; the seeds of the new heavens and a new earth where there is no more death or mourning or crying or pain. God plants the seeds of this glorious new reality with the invitation to Abram and Sarai to leave everything and everyone they've ever known and become immigrants in a land they had not yet seen. This courageous action was not just for them, but for the whole world.

And they say, "Yes."

Because they said yes to this journey, God gives Abram and Sarai new names and identities, sends them to a new land and a new family, and transforms their story.

And the world was changed because of it.

And the world will be changed because of it.

This story reveals a pattern we see throughout Scripture: God's transformative and redemptive work in our lives, and in the world, often happens when we're willing to leave home and embark on a journey.

It's as if God is saying, "If you don't go, you won't grow."

And while this truth is central to the biblical story, I think many of us as Christians naturally resist the invitation to "leave home," and in doing so, we miss out on participating in the work that God wants to do in us and through us.

DECENTERING THE MAP

Growing up in the Midwestern United States, the land where I lived was always at the center of every map I saw. In fact, I can't remember ever seeing a map from different times, locations, and cultures, where the people group that made the map didn't put their own location in the center. On the one hand, this is for very practical reasons. If you're leaving home and venturing into an unknown land, you need as much space as possible on the map to chart all that is around you. On the other hand, this is also a clear example of our tendency to see ourselves as the center of the world, as "normal," and to see everywhere, everything, and everyone else as "other," if for no other reason than it's all unknown. It is also a symptom of power, and often associated with domination or oppression of other groups.

We put ourselves at the middle of the map, and sometimes even ignore that there are other locations on the map or that there is more to be discovered and understood. We resist recognizing that our place, people, and beliefs may not be the center of the universe, and we resist exploring what lies beyond the safety of our tribe and location.

We often confuse our known place on the map for the entire map.

Or, more simply, we often confuse our known place on the map for the entire map.

I have found this to be true in my experience of Christianity and the church, especially in my work with young people. Like many of us who serve in youth ministry, I have experienced fear and anxiety as students have "left home." Sometimes this meant they literally went off to college, the military, or job training after high school. Other times they left metaphorically—stepped away from the beliefs, practices, and people who had previously been part of their lives. A few times this was a declared and vocal separation. Other times it was more of a process or slow drift. I have felt the grief and sadness that so many of us have when our young people walk away from us, and the consequences lead them to encounter struggle, pain, failure, and loss. There are few things worse than this experience as a youth worker, parent, and friend.

However, I've also been at this long enough now that I've been able to see a much longer arc in students' journeys. One of the gifts I've received the past few years is to hear back from students who graduated five, ten, or fifteen years ago. Despite my best efforts, it has been nearly impossible to track with all of them beyond their years in our high school ministry. When we reconnect, though, they've been eager to introduce their spouse or romantic interest, excited to tell me about their career (or lack thereof), and sometimes even about what they've experienced spiritually since the last time we had been together. While each of these interactions surely included some description of hardship, I've always walked away with an overwhelming sense of awe and gratitude for the kind of people they're becoming. All of this has caused me to reflect on how I think about the transition out of high school for our young people.

For many, they weren't just walking away from home. They were leaving the home of their childhood to begin building their own sense of home.

For many, they weren't just walking away from their faith. They were walking away from my faith, or the faith of their parents, or the faith of their childhood—which is why it all felt so personal to the rest of us.

They weren't walking off the map, they were just leaving the place they used to call home. They were leaving the place on the map they had previously occupied with us.

Once I realized the faith map is bigger than my location on it, my perspective on this entire process changed. Eventually their leaving began to seem like a natural part of how God intends to grow and shape all of us into the people God created us to be. To be clear, I am not prescribing that every student should walk away from their faith or church after high school. However, the steps that some students need to take to grow in their faith might actually *look like* walking away from their faith to others, whether that happens during high school or beyond.

Now, there's always the chance young people will end up in dangerous territory as they go on this journey. We all likely know young people for whom leaving home or stepping away from the faith of their childhood was a catastrophic endeavor, and I don't intend to minimize the pain and heartache experienced by everyone involved. I have experienced this heartache myself. But I am convinced it's just as bad—and maybe even worse—to never leave "home," and therefore never find a home or beliefs of their own.

WHAT IS THE BIBLE AND HOW DO WE READ IT?

I have found all of this to be directly related to conversations about how we read the Bible.

Throughout much of Christian history, and especially in the past one hundred years, there has been a lot of time and energy spent on answering the question, "What is the Bible?" At its best, this question has led countless people to read and re-read, and to consider and reconsider, what the Bible says that it is and what historic Christian communities have said about it. It has also led people, churches, and denominations to come up with formal statements and detailed positions on the nature of the Bible. This is often where the words "inspired," "authoritative," and "inerrant" enter the conversation. These words, and the words that come with them, have brought clear definition to those who've desired it on what the Bible is and its place in the Christian life. In so many ways, this has been a necessary and helpful venture.

At its worst, however, the question of, "What is the Bible?" has led to argument and division. Rather than leading to a growing imagination and broader perspective of "the map," the question has caused many to hunker down on certainty, circle the wagons on theological purity, and in some cases, insist that their place on the map is actually the entire map. This is, in part, how we've ended up with thousands of Christian denominations in the United States alone, many of which are claiming to be the only place on the map rather than recognizing the beauty, diversity, and nuance that a larger map—a broader view of Christianity and the spiritual journey—would offer. This sort of mindset is common in many of our beliefs and traditions. It has certainly been part of the colonialist enterprise, but none of us are immune to participating in these sorts of narrowing behaviors.

When our young people "walk away," it might be because they consciously or subconsciously know that there is more to be explored and encountered in the journey of faith. Abraham and Sarah's faith may not have seemed so stable to the families they left behind, but this turned out to be a pilgrimage of deep faithfulness.

Our young people might know better than us that if they want to grow, they have to go.

For all the good and all the bad that has come from our attempts to clearly articulate, "What is the Bible?", for many of us this process hasn't directly led to answering the practical question of, "How should we read it?"—which is the primary task of this book.

This book is mostly a map of my journey with youth ministry and the Bible. It is a reflection of over a decade of serving in pastoral ministry, while also studying the Bible in college and in graduate school from a diversity of perspectives and traditions in North America, Turkey, Israel, Egypt, and Jordan. Every step along the way offers the tools and ideas that previously had been unfamiliar to me when it comes to encountering the Bible in my own life and with my students. Each chapter of this book is meant to be experienced like a stop, stage, or "place" on the journey—which might also be your journey. In my pilgrimage with the Bible, I've spent time in the locations of:

- A Book to Read

- Commands to Obey

- A Land to Experience

- A Way to Live

- A Story to Engage

- Questions to Ask

- A Wrestling Match

- A Prayer Book

This is the order of my progression, journey, and growth as a follower of Jesus and as a pastor. It is in no way comprehensive of how all Christians read the Bible, but each of these stops connects to aspects of the Christian tradition that I discovered along the path, and that deeply impacted my work with young people. Each stop along the way felt like a "new home," or a point of arrival, until I was beckoned to consider that once again, the map is bigger than I had considered, and that there is more to experience on my journey. This journey has not been an easy one. It has been filled with a messy combination of joy and pain, success and failure, laughter and tears, and intentional and unintentional discoveries. Every step along the way has presented its own challenges.

Each stop along the way felt like a "new home," or a point of arrival, until I was beckoned to consider that once again, the map is bigger than I had considered, and that there is more to experience on my journey.

I recognize that in so many ways, my story was born out of a place of privilege, and that privilege has enabled me to embark on a journey that many others will never have the opportunity to experience. That privilege has also blinded me to stops along the way that I should have been making in order to keep growing. As Fuller Seminary's Keon-Sang An has noted, "People's social location provides the perspective from and in which they see and understand the biblical texts."[1] This is why our collective journeys are so important, because the map won't be complete until we're all sharing our stories, discoveries, and traditions with one another.

My hope is that this map feels like an invitation to consider venturing outside your comfort zone and tradition, too. Whether you're a veteran youth worker or you're just getting started, I hope it provides some tools to help you on your journey. Maybe, like me, you've wondered:

Is there more than one way to read the Bible?

Is there more than one way to study the Bible in our youth ministry?

How can we engage students with the Bible in a way that they'll want to keep reading it?

What do we do with all of our students' questions about what we read in the Bible?

Given historical context and nuance, which commands in the Bible are we supposed to tell students to obey today?

How can engaging the Bible be a spiritual experience, not just an educational exercise?

Or, the question we're all asking: *What should we do at youth group next week?*

If you've asked any of those questions, or other leaders

---

1 Keon-Sang An, "The Contextual Nature of Biblical Interpretation: An Ethiopian Case," *Fuller Magazine* issue 8 (2017), 38. Here "social location" includes "both the location of a society and an individual's position in the society," which all influence our interpretive practices.

in your ministry have struggled to know how to open the Bible with young people in small groups, Sunday school, mentoring relationships, or through camps and retreats, this book is for you.

We're on this journey together.

1

A
BOOK
TO
READ

HOW IS YOUR RELATIONSHIP
WITH THE BIBLE?

*If your Instruction hadn't been my delight, I would
have died because of my suffering. I will never
forget your precepts.*

PSALM 119:92-93

MY FIRST LOOK AT THE GOOD BOOK

"I just want to kill myself."

I stammered through these words, choking on my own tears, while driving my friend to school. Up until a few days ago, this friend had been my girlfriend. It was a sunny day, and the morning light made it even more difficult for my swollen eyes to see through my tears.

I was seventeen years old, a senior in high school, and in the middle of making decisions about college, career, relationships, and what seemed like the rest of my life.

My girlfriend had just broken up with me.

My coach cut me from the basketball team.

Nothing seemed to be fitting together the way it seemed to for others. My breaths were short and my feet felt heavy. I didn't know who I was, who my friends were, or what I was supposed to be doing with my life. Looking back, I know I was struggling with anxiety and depression, and ideally my parents, friends, and teachers would have been better equipped to see the signs and connect me to the help I needed.

I was one of the few people in West Michigan who didn't grow up going to church and with Jesus explicitly at the forefront of every part of my life. To be clear, I was raised in a loving family with remarkable parents and an awesome younger brother. From the outside looking in, we probably seemed like a Christian family. We just didn't ever go to church on Sunday and didn't put Jesus stickers on everything. In fact, I don't remember us ever really talking about Jesus as a family, and I had never opened a Bible.

Growing up without Jesus and the Bible had been working just fine for me. I was perfectly happy sleeping in on Sunday and watching the Detroit Lions. (Ironically, growing up as a Lions fan prepared me to understand and participate in the season of Lent later in life—they are a historically bad football team.) My family and my life still contained love and meaning.

But in this moment of honesty with my ex-girlfriend that morning, I was struggling through much more than just normal teenage angst. She was the first person I had told about my dark thoughts, and I think she could tell.

She looked at me and said, "You need Jesus. I want you to come to church with me on Sunday."

All I heard was the invitation to go somewhere with her, which highly interested me, even if it meant going to church. She was the one who had dumped me, and I was the fool who still liked her so much I was giving her a ride to school.

The following Sunday I joined her for church. I was nervous that my clothes weren't nice enough and that I wouldn't understand the version of English these people would be speaking. I assumed there was some way that people who went to church could tell immediately if you had never been to church before, and that this moment would involve a lot of shame, judgment, and embarrassment. Taking the leap to visit a church wasn't calming my anxiety at all.

Once we arrived, I found some people I recognized from school and began to talk with them, and they seemed genuinely happy to see me. I felt embraced by the new people I met, and my anxiety began to decrease. The conversations were interrupted by musicians beginning to play, and people seemed instinctively to know it was time to stop what they were doing and find seats. After several songs that were completely unfamiliar to me but well known to everyone else, an enthusiastic man in a white shirt and black pants jumped on stage and invited us to turn to the book of Leviticus. Apparently, this was part of the Bible.

People were walking up and down the aisles passing out Bibles to anyone who needed one. I raised my hand and someone sent a book my way.

While holding my breath, I somehow was able to find the correct place in the Bible by following the page numbers and passage references projected on a large screen in the front of the room.

And for the first time in my life, at age seventeen, I cracked open this book, the Bible, and began reading.

The pastor made several jokes about the book of Leviticus being a strange place to begin a sermon, which I didn't understand until I actually started reading. If you're not familiar with Leviticus, it is filled with instructions about temple worship, ritual sacrifice, dietary laws, and other obscure guidelines for the ancient religious worship of the Israelites. I was immediately lost.

The sermon started in Leviticus, but progressed from the front of the Bible, where Leviticus is located, all way through to what seemed like near the end of the Bible, to the Gospel of John. Each passage we looked up would have been confusing if I were reading on my own, but the explanation provided by the pastor not only made sense of the parts of the Bible we were reading, it also intersected with my life in a way that sparked curiosity. Somehow, all these passages fit together and seemed invitational and compelling.

While my first experience at church impacted me in several significant ways, it primarily provoked a curiosity about the Bible that was unexplainable to me at the time. My ex-girlfriend who brought me to church that morning later purchased a Bible for me, and over the next several months I kept going to church on my own and reading the Bible every moment I could. I started carrying it around during the day and reading it between classes and during free time at school, even staying up late at night reading.

Most of what I was reading didn't make sense, but there was something about it that kept pulling me further and further in.

I couldn't put it down.

After just a few months, I had read the entire New Testament several times and had begun working my way through the Old Testament. Most of what I was reading didn't make sense, but there was something about it that kept pulling me further and further in.

The Bible was satisfying me while also leaving me wanting

more in the best possible way.

But it was doing more than satisfying me.

The Bible was saving me.

It was saving me from my despair, and pointing me to something, and someone, that offered so much more than I had ever experienced before. And all of the friends I made at church encouraged me to keep it up.

Keep reading.

Just keep reading.

Before I had a relationship with Jesus, I discovered a connection with the Bible. I have often described this season of my life as the beginning of my "personal relationship with the Bible." And while I knew nothing about doctrine or words like inerrant, infallible, or inspired, I was falling in love with the stories and poems that portrayed the loving relationship others have had with this book throughout history.

Little did I know this relationship would shape the next twenty years of my life in ways I couldn't have imagined.

FROM YOUTH TO YOUTH WORKER

Just under seven years after my first experience at church and my first time reading the Bible, I found myself leading a high school ministry at a large church with over one hundred adult volunteers and many more students. The story of how I accidentally became a youth pastor is one for another day, but I was excited about working with high school students, and even more excited about sharing my love for the Bible with them.

However, I hit some massive speed bumps right out of the gate.

All of my passion and excitement about the Bible was met with discomfort, nervousness, and even some embarrassment. Most of my students had grown up in church and many went to Christian school, and yet the majority of them were admittedly completely unfamiliar with the Bible. They lacked the confidence to open it or read it on their own.

Despite attempting to remedy this during my first four years serving in youth ministry, this lack of confidence came to fruition one spring at our senior retreat. In the midst of sharing hopes and fears about the coming season of life, one of our more reserved students vulnerably shared, "I'm actually just really afraid. I'm afraid that I don't have all of the Bible verses I need to make it through this summer and into my first semester of college. I don't know where to find them."

There was a sense of agreement in the room from the other students and leaders. His honesty created space for everyone else to acknowledge they had the same feelings. Aside from empathy for the fear and insecurity expressed by this student, I also experienced a sense of devastation and disappointment.

Despite four years in our high school ministry, and all my best efforts, this student believed there were verses in the Bible about how to survive your first year out of high school and he was scared he didn't know where to find them. He didn't really know what the Bible was about or what kind of content it actually contained. As a mature and intelligent eighteen-year-old who would be moving out of state to attend an academically rigorous university, he was essentially confessing he still needed a pastor to spoon-feed him the Bible. This student loved Jesus and loved the church and was the sort of kid every youth pastor wishes to have, yet he didn't have any idea how to read the Bible on his own.

This student loved Jesus and loved the church and was the sort of kid every youth pastor wishes to have, yet he didn't have any idea how to read the Bible on his own.

But this isn't just the story of my students and my youth group.

According to the Sticky Faith research conducted by the Fuller Youth Institute, at the end of high school, only 42 percent of students in youth groups said they read the Bible weekly, and only 12 percent read their Bibles daily.[1] In other words, significantly less than half of our youth group graduates are

1 Kara Powell, Brad M. Griffin, and Cheryl Crawford, *Sticky Faith Youth Worker Edition: Practical Ideas to Nurture Long-Term Faith in Teenagers,* (Grand Rapids: Zondervan, 2011), 143. See fulleryouthinstitute.org/stickyfaith.

reading the Bible more than once each week.

But before we all start lamenting the apparent biblical illiteracy of today's young people, it's worth saying that what also surprised me during my first season as a high school pastor was this: Despite the declared love for the Bible among most of our adult volunteers, many of them were also uncomfortable with Scripture, and felt inadequate opening and reading a Bible with students. In fact, many of my volunteers actively resisted my attempts to set them up to do this well.

They wanted our teaching to be "Bible-based," they wanted the curriculum to teach "biblical values," but when I wanted them to actually read the Bible with students, I often received blank stares. When I asked students after their small group meeting each week if they opened their Bibles together as a group, they usually replied, "No."

I don't believe that young people are uninterested in reading the Bible—they just don't know how. My experience tells me that most adults are not equipped to cultivate this interest among students. Most of the adult volunteers and students I know who aren't comfortable with opening and reading the Bible have never had someone model it, do it with them, and let them try it in the context of a relationship.

They've never been mentored or apprenticed in this area of their faith.

And they're also likely feeling somewhere between insecure and embarrassed about it. Maybe you can relate.

While every church and youth group is different, I don't think this reality was unique to the youth ministry I was leading. Despite youth ministry's propensity to tape Bible verses on every wall, website, brochure, and T-shirt, many of us haven't created cultures in our youth ministries where Bible reading is as familiar as dodgeball and pizza.

And when opening the Bible actually seems too scary, the temptation is just to play more games and eat more snacks.

I'm not advocating that we change all of our youth gatherings into two-hour Bible studies, and I don't think that normalizing Bible reading in our youth group has to come at the expense of fun.

Nor do I think studying the Bible with young people has to mean more proof-texting

or

more forced Scripture memorization

or

more "making the Bible relevant" (as if we're the ones "making" the Bible into something)

or

more "read the Bible and it will fix all of your problems"

or

more "here are the ten verses on why you shouldn't do drugs"

or

more "if you're not reading the Bible you're not a real

Christian" sort of shaming

or

more "let me tell you what the Bible means."

Instead, I'm talking about normalizing reading the Bible in your life and in your ministry. I'm not talking about anything other than considering that the Bible is a book worth reading, and inviting your students to immerse themselves in this book and its stories. As a seventeen-year-old senior in high school, simply being invited into a relationship with the Bible saved my life by introducing me to the God whose story it tells, and I believe this simple invitation could save the lives of others as well.

In ministry, I came to realize that one of the most important tasks I'd have as a high school pastor would be to continue to normalize Bible reading as part of my own life, as a part of our ministry culture, and hopefully as a part of the lives of our volunteers and students.

And if I had to guess, I bet you have some work to do on this, too.

Every time you're with your students and other leaders, you have the opportunity to model the practice of reading the Bible. Every time you're giving a talk, leading a small group, or hosting a training, you have the opportunity to apprentice individuals and your entire community toward growing their own relationship with the Bible.

Even if you're not in charge of your youth ministry, your personal practice of reading the Bible and your willingness to apprentice others can influence a ministry culture of

Bible reading. My spiritual journey began with reading this book we call the Bible, and this is likely the most helpful starting point, or restarting point, for you and the young people with whom you've been entrusted.

"Formed by our reading of Scripture, we become better readers of Scripture. This is not because we become better skilled at applying biblical principles. The practice of reading Scripture is not about learning how to mold the biblical message to contemporary lives and modern needs. Rather, the Scriptures yearn to reshape how we comprehend our lives and identify our greatest needs. We find in Scripture who we are and what we might become, so that we come to share its assessment of our situation, encounter its promise of restoration, and hear its challenge to serve God's good news."

—JOEL B. GREEN[2]

---

2 Joel B. Green, "Cultivating the Practice of Reading Scripture," Catalyst resources, http://www.catalystresources.org/cultivating-the-practice-of-reading-scripture/. Emphasis added. Also see Green's *Seized by Truth: Reading the Bible as Scripture* (Nashville: Abingdon, 2007).

SO, HOW'S YOUR PERSONAL RELATIONSHIP WITH THE BIBLE?

If you're serving as a youth worker or grew up in the church, you may have experienced seasons in your life when you couldn't put the Bible down. You may have had a sense of "that's me!" when you read the story of my growing "personal relationship with the Bible." It's likely you're one of the countless people over thousands of years who just couldn't stop reading. And you read and you read and you read and you loved it.

It's also possible that you grew up in a church culture or work in an environment where, because you read and you read and you read, you don't love it like you once did. Or possibly you were never given the opportunity to love it because of the way you were taught to read it. Perhaps Scripture has been used in your life in a way that causes fear or confusion.

For some of you, reading this book may be as close as you've been to desiring to actually read the Bible. And we all can picture the faces of our students who haven't demonstrated a hunger to dive into the words of Scripture. Regardless of where you or your students are, or where you're coming from in your own relationship with the Bible, actually reading it is the necessary starting or restarting point on this journey. If you want the young people who have been entrusted to your care to have a deep and meaningful relationship with the Bible, then that starts with you.

Have you ever had a leader or volunteer in your youth ministry who always listened to a specific rap artist or followed a certain sports team, and in a short amount of time all of the young people that person led or spent time with suddenly started listening to that rapper or following that sports team? Funny how that works, isn't it? Or, if you're a youth worker and you have a spouse or partner or kids, don't your students know about them? Don't they desire to become more familiar with them, even if it's from a distance?

Why does this happen?

It's because we can't help but share the things and the people we love with others.

If something or someone is a meaningful part of your life, others will take notice and follow.

What is influencing you will inevitably influence others.

So how is your own relationship with the Bible these days? Is it time for you to dust off that book on your nightstand and begin again?

If yes, I want to encourage you to start reading.

Keep reading.

Don't stop reading.

And if you read, eventually, they will too.

TRY THIS ... IN YOUR LIFE:

- Purchase a new Bible, preferably a translation you've never read so that familiar words and stories will seem new and fresh, and start reading!

- Find an audio version of the Bible, and make a commitment to listen whenever you're driving, exercising, washing dishes, before bed, etc., for a season.

- Find an online Bible reading plan that isn't overly ambitious, but will stretch you into new habits.

- Tell your pastor or supervisor that you want to try to cultivate a culture of Bible reading in your ministry, and that needs to start in your own life. Ask for support and accountability to make Bible reading part of your daily "work."

- Don't always read the Bible alone. Ask some friends or colleagues to join you on this journey. Meeting together to read the Bible with one another on a semi-regular basis, or reading the same Scriptures even if you're not together, will encourage you and hold you accountable.

- View reading the Bible as a relationship. There will be good days and bad days. All you can do is create opportunities and environments where you can fall in love (maybe for the second or third time).

TRY THIS ... IN YOUR MINISTRY:

- Don't assume your students and leaders have their own Bible. Ask them if they do and offer to provide one if they don't.

- Invite your team to bring their own Bible to youth group each week. Not just a mobile app version, but a paper version. Our brains encode thoughts and memories differently when we read, turn, and mark physical pages.

- Invite students to bring their own Bibles each week.

- As you teach, only list Bible verse references in your presentations and on the screen, rather than entire passages. Have plenty of extra Bibles for guests and those who forgot them and invite students and volunteers to actually turn to the verses you want to read in their Bibles, and teach them how to find them.

- Teach from your own Bible.

- As you teach and lead, share your own struggles with reading the Bible ["this was/is confusing to me," "this is a strange story," "I used to think this was boring," etc.].

- Make daily Bible readings available to your students and volunteers via website/social media/apps, etc. Not all will do it, but for some, your making it available is all they need to get going.

- Explain to parents why this is important for the formation of their kids' faith, and invite them on this journey as well.

2

COMMANDS TO OBEY

WHAT IS THE BIBLE ASKING OF US?

So love the LORD your God and follow his instruction, his regulations, his case laws, and his commandments always.

DEUTERONOMY 11:1

I READ AND I READ

During my first twelve months as a Christian, my curiosity about the Bible turned into an unquenchable passion for learning as much as I possibly could about this book. I remember someone giving me a commentary on the book of Romans, and since I didn't know what a commentary was or how it worked, I read it from cover to cover.

If you're just getting started with the Bible, I would not recommend this method.

But I just couldn't stop reading.

During this time, I went from a confused high school senior to a graduate about to change all of his college plans to attend a school where he could learn more about his faith, and maybe even become a pastor.

When I told one of my new church friends that I thought I might want to become a pastor, she suggested I apply to a Bible school a few hours from home. I didn't realize there were countless schools in the world that would provide me with the Bible education and training I needed to prepare to be a pastor. In fact, there were several of these types of schools in my hometown. I just didn't know about them because I was new at this whole Bible-Church-Jesus thing. So, I applied to the only Bible school I had ever heard of.

As I read more about the school and dug into the application, I noticed that there were many pages spent explaining what the school believed, what students were expected to believe, and what appropriate behavior and conduct looked like for current and prospective students.

All of these expectations were organized in lists, and each list item had a Bible verse in parentheses at the end.

I sorted through detailed descriptions of the Trinity, rules forbidding going to a movie theater, details of a dress code, a position about the validity of speaking in tongues, specifics about how the world will end, strict guidelines on what dancing is and isn't and why students can't do any of it, the color of the tie the antichrist will be wearing when he arrives,[1] and explanations about appropriate relationships with the opposite gender.

I remember being impressed, and thinking, "These people have it figured out."

They were getting the most mileage out of the Bible of anyone I had ever seen. It seemed as though every question about even the most practical aspects of being a godly college student could be addressed with at least one Bible verse; sometimes more.

This school seemed to know what each of those verses meant, and they weren't afraid to use them.

I found this approach to life fascinating. For someone as in love with the Bible as I was, a place that had immersed every aspect of life in the Bible was really compelling to me, even though I didn't completely understand all of the implications of the rules.

Many of the rules pushed against my upbringing and the way I lived my life. I wondered why none of my new Christian friends had ever explained any of this really

---

1 This wasn't actually in the application form. The rest of this list is real.

important stuff to me since it was, according to this school, so clearly what the Bible said.

So, I wrote about all of that in my application essays. I was honest about how silly or confusing I thought some of the school's rules were. I told myself my lack of understanding had to do with my lack of familiarity with the Bible and how Christians were supposed to act, but looking back, this was my first small act of rebellion against the rules. Yet eventually I received my acceptance to the school.

When I arrived the following August, it felt like visiting a new and amazing universe that I never even knew existed. Everyone on campus loved the Bible and wanted to serve in ministry, and that's all we talked about. I loved it. I don't think I blinked or stopped smiling for a week.

During that first week of school my roommate asked me if I wanted to try to memorize the book of Philippians with him and be his "accountability partner." I said yes, even though I wasn't sure what any of that meant.[2] I really just wanted him to teach me how to iron my clothes the way he did (but I was afraid to ask).

I learned about "devotions" and "dating" and "dispensations" and "honoring God" and "systematic theology" and how to win any argument by using the word "biblical." I discovered it was normal for strangers to ask you questions about your spiritual background and upbringing— that was just part of how Christians talked with each other in this particular subculture.

---

2 Later I found out it just meant we would talk about not looking at pornography.

During my first few weeks, I absorbed all the spoken and unspoken rules of how this world worked. I did my best to bend my life toward this new way of living. I loved the Bible, after all, and I was learning that this way of life was "biblical."

UNTIL I STOPPED READING

One Tuesday morning during the first month of school, I took the elevator down to the main floor of my dorm where there was one of the few televisions on campus. As the elevator doors opened, I looked up and saw, on the television screen mounted on the wall, a giant building collapsing. It was the first tower of the World Trade Center falling down on the streets of New York City.

September 11, 2001, and the days following, sent me over the edge. The chaos of this event became fertilizer for any seeds of rebellion that were already planted in my heart.

Every time I closed my eyes, I saw the scenes from that day: TV news shots of streets jammed with cars trying to evacuate the city, the silence of my school's normally loud and chaotic dining hall, and students wandering around campus crying. I felt homesick, and I would have done anything just to be with my family and my church community.

The well-intentioned words offered by students and professors did little to comfort me. It didn't feel like "God was in control," that "God had a special blessing on

America," that "war was now justified," or that "prayer and obedience should be our focus." It didn't matter to me anymore that they offered plenty of Bible verses to support these statements.

I was nineteen years old, living away from home for the first time, and trying to figure out how to cope with a national tragedy on my own. I had never been an undisciplined person, but I always went where the energy and life was. I was in the midst of coming down from a two-year spiritual adrenaline rush and all I knew in that moment was fear, pain, and confusion. Everything seemed absurd, and after a month of being at Bible school, I was done with all of the rules, requirements, and expectations.

So, I found other people like me and we became friends.

I stopped sleeping at night and started napping between lunch and dinner.

I stayed out past curfew and figured out how to sneak back on campus without getting caught.

I attended chapel to meet the requirement but slept in the balcony while my RA tried to keep me awake.

I "lofted" my bed two inches off the floor, only because it was against the rules.

I took a job working the front desk of my dorm so I could let people in past curfew.

A friend and I planned spontaneous dance parties around campus.

I abandoned my accountability partnership with my roommate and didn't memorize one verse from Philippians.

I began to hate people who seemed to be doing just fine or fitting in with the culture and the rules.

I coasted through the first semester academically, jumping through the hoops and meeting the minimum requirements, while somehow achieving decent grades.

One evening I was in the lounge on our dorm floor and I overheard one guy telling another guy that he felt guilty for "not being in the Word" as much as he should be. Only a few months earlier I wouldn't have known what this meant, yet I had quickly sunk to a cynical place where a statement like this would cause me to roll my eyes.

But this time it didn't.

It felt like someone had slid a mirror right in front of my face, and it was painfully uncomfortable for me to look. I walked back to my room and realized that it had been several months since I had opened and read my Bible. In the midst of all of my intentional rebellion against the rules, I had unintentionally stopped reading the book that I loved.

The love and passion that I had for learning about the Bible, my desire to teach it to others, and the entire reason I was at that school had gone off the rails. While I wasn't spending my evenings at clubs, using drugs, or hooking up with girls, I was living in intentional rebellion to the rules of the school I had chosen to attend and to the commitment I had made to myself, others, and God. I had confused the rules of the school with the Bible, so I dismissed both.

I had confused the rules of the school with the Bible, so I dismissed both.

I had come to Bible school because I wanted to "master the Bible," but I realized that the Bible wanted to master me. And during this season of my life, it became clear that if I was going to follow Jesus, just reading the Bible wasn't enough.

The Bible was asking something of me.

This is one of the most painful and difficult realities I've ever had to accept, and most of my lifestyle needed to change.

MORE THAN READING

One of the more familiar stories in the Bible is the story of God rescuing the Israelites from slavery in Egypt in the book of Exodus. In the Hebrew tradition, this story is *the story*. It is the central narrative of the Jewish people. For Christians, the life, death, resurrection, and ascension of Jesus is seen as both the climax to, while also a retelling of, this great redemptive event.

After God rescues the Israelites from Egypt, and before they receive Torah (or God's commandments), they find themselves encamped at the foot of a mountain in the wilderness of Sinai. Both Exodus and Deuteronomy record versions of this event, and what the text shows us is sort of like the telephone game, where Moses plays the role of the "go-between" for God and the Israelites. Moses represents the Israelite people while talking to God at the top of the mountain, and represents God while talking to the Israelites at the bottom of the mountain.

After Moses' first trip up the mountain, he returns to the camp and shares the words of God with the people. The Israelites respond:

"Everything that the LORD has said we will do." (Exodus 19:8)

And

"We will listen and obey." (Deuteronomy 5:27, NIV)

These passages mark a turning point in the story of the relationship between God and God's people, and they provide depth and insight as to how we read the Bible.

God's words demand a response.

There is an inherent reaction expected in the revealing of God's words to the people of God.

God's words are to be more than just heard or read.

If we're actually going to learn and if we're actually going to grow, our response must be that of the Israelites:

We will read AND we will obey.

We will do what you're telling us to do.

One of the first invitations to genuine growth and transformation is to understand that God is asking something of us. The spiritual journey will cost us something. And, for many of us, the cost will initially feel like too much.

It did for the Israelites, so God started with the basics (see Exodus 20):

"Don't worship other gods."

"Stop killing each other."

"Take a day off once a week."

In our modern world, much of this seems like common sense, but imagine living in a world where this would have been new information or a set of groundbreaking ideas.

The Israelites understood that if they were going to live into the story God was inviting them to, there were certain guidelines they would have to follow. God was blessing them and taking care of them, but God was also asking something of them. God was asking for radical obedience to Torah.

And God is asking something of each of us. One of the basic beliefs of the Christian tradition is that the Bible reveals what God is asking of us. While it seems that most Christians agree this is true, there is not much agreement on what this obedience actually looks like. Different streams of the Christian tradition have named and interpreted it in different ways.

I have friends who love Jesus, and who have wholeheartedly devoted their lives to following all 613 commandments of the Torah.

I have friends who love Jesus and spend all of their time

and energy emphasizing radical obedience to the Sermon on the Mount in Matthew 5-7.

One of my mentors, who loved Jesus more than anyone I know, consistently boiled everything in life down to "the Greatest Commandment" (Matthew 22:34-40). He believed that loving God and loving our neighbor was all that God specifically asks of us.

When the Pharisees heard that Jesus had left the Sadducees speechless, they met together. One of them, a legal expert, tested him. "Teacher, what is the greatest commandment in the Law?"

He replied, "You must love the Lord your God with all your heart, with all your being, and with all your mind. This is the first and greatest commandment. And the second is like it: You must love your neighbor as you love yourself. All the Law and the Prophets depend on these two commands."

MATTHEW 22:34-40

I have heard many other people say things like:

"A disciplined life is a godly life."

And

"Our level of obedience displays our level of gratitude."

And

"Our faithfulness to God is measured by our willingness to live righteous lives."

For my roommate in college, answering the question, "What is the Bible asking of me?" looked liked early morning Bible reading and prayer, perfectly pressed shirts, going to bed on time, and studying diligently for class.

For others, answering this question can look very different.

Regardless of your tradition or how you hammer out the specifics, I am convinced that the Bible is not just a book to be read—it is also a set of commands to be obeyed.

The Bible is asking something of you.

And it is asking something of your students as well.

HOW DO I KNOW WHICH COMMANDS TO OBEY?

In Matthew 22:34-40 the Pharisees ask Jesus, "Teacher, which is the greatest commandment in the Law?" By asking this question, they were trying to lead Jesus into a theological minefield. Many religious teachers during this time period had their own ranking of the 613 commandments. Prioritizing laws was helpful because some of the rules could be contradictory depending on the context. As you can imagine, there was much disagreement over the order in which the commandments should be prioritized. Jesus responds by linking Deuteronomy 6:4 with Leviticus 19:18 as #1 and #2 of 613, which wouldn't have been an uncommon response to this question. It also reveals Jesus' theological agenda.

You might be thinking, "It's so hard for me to imagine a world where well-intentioned religious people argue and debate the meaning of the Bible and what obedience looks like." Of course, I am being sarcastic. Differing interpretations have been around as long as Scripture, and there has never been a shortage of passionate people willing to jump into the conversation to debate these interpretations. Questions about specific traditions, denominations, and interpretations; the difference between timeless and temporal truths; and what faithfulness in your life looks like; these are age-old questions that we can't answer in this short book.

However, what we can acknowledge is that most often at the heart of these questions and debates resides a deep love for God and the Bible and a genuine desire to live faithful and obedient lives. In Acts 15:28 we read that even when engaging in an important and heated debate, the early church crafted their conclusion with the opening line, "It seemed good to us and to the Holy Spirit." This posture requires significant humility and the recognition that the work of interpretation isn't a prelude to obedience, but is actually part of our obedience. Moses, Deborah, Mary, Jesus, Paul, and the early church participated in this sort of process, and so do we, whether we realize it or not.

Welcome to the conversation.

THE GOSPEL OF SIN MANAGEMENT MIGHT ACTUALLY BE GOOD NEWS ... SORT OF

If you're reading this book, you might be familiar with the terms "behavior modification" and "the gospel of sin management."[3] These terms have become common vernacular in many youth ministry conversations, and are often leveled as a critique of the messages we inadvertently communicate to our young people: God primarily wants you to change how you're acting and to better manage your sins. These messages are obviously lacking, and cut to the heart of what many of us already know to be true. If all the spiritual life offers us is a path to "sin a little less," not only is that uninteresting, it's also radically ineffective in experiencing long-term transformation.

But here's what I've come to realize: behavior change is part of the biblical story and actually an essential part of our own spiritual growth. It was certainly an essential part of the spiritual growth of the people of God.[4]

---

3 I first read about the "gospel of sin management" in the late Dallas Willard's excellent book, *The Divine Conspiracy: Rediscovering Our Hidden Life In God* (New York: HarperCollins, 1998). For more on this in a youth ministry context, explore the "Sticky Faith" resources by the Fuller Youth Institute. See fulleryouthinstitute.org/stickyfaith.

4 There have been a number of books written on what on earth Paul is talking about in Galatians. I think behavior change is, in part, what Paul is getting at in Galatians 3:24. The idea is that there are seasons in our life and development, spiritual and otherwise, when we need rules in order

For clarity, I don't believe the "gospel of sin management" is actually the Gospel, and I don't think behavior modification is the ultimate destination of the spiritual life. Behavior change is, however, part of the journey.

When God says, "Don't murder!" and the Israelites say, "We will listen and obey," what is actually happening here? God is commanding the Israelites to change how they're living, to "modify their behavior," and the Israelites are willing to commit to giving it a try.

As someone who would like not to be murdered, I find this sort of behavior modification to be quite helpful.

And it can be for your students, too.

We can all agree that "don't kill each other" is a good rule to follow, but most of life's circumstances, as well as the biblical text, feel less clear and more complex than this commandment. Reading Scripture through a lens of behavior modification is not only easy to abuse, it is likely already the most prevalent interpretation in our communities, which is part of why a number of today's youth ministry leaders have reacted so strongly against it.

---

to learn and grow. Once we exist in relationship with these rules, we can begin to differentiate from them and enter a new season of growth. I think Paul is saying something like, "You needed the rules for a season, but now you're able to enter into a true relationship with the living God that transcends these rules through Jesus." How does that interpretation line up with your own tradition or your understanding of commands in Scripture?

LEARNING TO LOVE THE COMMANDS

When I first started in youth ministry, I struggled because I didn't want my students to believe that God would love them more if they followed rules or lived pure lives. This was their default mindset about God; it's what many of them had heard in church and in their homes their entire lives. But this is not what Jesus ever taught and is bad Christian theology.[5]

We didn't want our ministry to be one more voice lost in the crowd of voices screaming at them every day, and we for sure didn't want them to see God in that crowd.

I was also shocked by the demands placed on students in every area of their lives. I was less than a decade older than many of them, yet their reality seemed completely different than the one I had experienced as a teen. Later, this experience was helpfully framed by the work of Chap Clark, whose thesis is that today's young people are facing historically high expectations with a historically low level of

5 If you're not familiar with the phrase "Moralistic Therapeutic Deism," I highly recommend reading Kenda Creasy Dean's *Almost Christian: What the Faith of Our Teenagers is Telling the American Church* (New York: Oxford University Press, 2010).

adult support.[6] We didn't want our ministry to be one more voice lost in the crowd of voices screaming at them every day, and we for sure didn't want them to see God in that crowd.

So, I overcorrected in response to both of these realities, and the way I taught from the Bible asked very little of my students. On the one hand, this overcorrection felt pastorally appropriate and was likely needed during this season of their lives. On the other hand, incomplete theology is never a helpful response to bad theology.

It was around this time that my wife and I were living in a shared housing community with two other couples. One of the couples was a retired pastor and his wife. He had recently started a project of trying to take literally and seriously the teachings of Jesus and the early church, and he spent several months scouring the New Testament for commands and exhortations. He invited me on this journey with him, and I spent many weeks reading and underlining every command.

I didn't even make it to the Epistles before I was completely overwhelmed. People who say that "the Old Testament is about rules and the New Testament is about grace" haven't read the New Testament carefully. Jesus and the Apostles have no problem dishing out commands and exhortations left and right. Their teachings were and are clearly asking something of us.

I realized that I needed to strike a better balance between

---

6 Dr. Chap Clark's *Hurt 2.0: Inside the World of Today's Teenagers* (Grand Rapids: Baker Academic, 2011) completely changed how I practice youth ministry.

teaching our students that God loves them just as they are and also loves them too much to allow them to stay that way.

I wanted them to know that nothing in life worth having is easy or comes without a cost, and that you can't follow Jesus without it costing you something. Just the same, you can't read the Bible without it asking something of you.

So, what might it look like for the pendulum to stop swinging and for us to engage the Bible's instructions and commands in a healthy and honest way?

FOUR CRUCIAL QUESTIONS TO HELP STUDENTS CONSIDER WHAT THE BIBLE IS ASKING OF THEM

If you're going to ask your students to enter into a relationship with the Bible, it won't be long before what they're reading begins to create dissonance in their lives. They will eventually be confronted with the reality that the Bible is asking something of them, and that may be painful to accept. We as youth workers have the opportunity and privilege to guide them through this experience, but we will have to choose how and if we're willing to enter into these muddy conversations.

Perhaps the best way to read the rules within the Bible is to allow the rules to move beyond reading our *behavior* to reading our *hearts*.

When I was in college and volunteering as a high school ministry volunteer, I would meet a couple of guys from my small group every Sunday night at a local coffee shop. They called it "the group with no name," because, well, our group didn't have a name. But every Sunday morning I'd get a call from these guys (because texting wasn't a thing yet) to confirm whether or not "the group with no name" was meeting. As often as I was able, I'd answer, "Yes."

We would all bring homework to work on, but most often we ended up spending the time laughing and discussing the larger issues of their lives. While they didn't always bring their Bibles with them, they were earnestly seeking questions and answers on if, how, and why the Bible matters. They were hypersensitive to clichés and legalism, and they wanted something more than Jesus bumper stickers and youth group T-shirts. There is a church on nearly every corner in West Michigan, and during this time many communities were trying to make it as easy as possible for students to follow Jesus and identify with the church. While well-intentioned and helpful to many young people, this approach wasn't working with these high school boys or with their friends.

It left me wondering, is it possible that our attempts to make the message of the Bible attractive and relevant are also the reasons our students find the Bible uninteresting? Is it possible that our young people don't respond to the Bible because we haven't helped them see that the Bible asks something of them?

Is it possible that our attempts to make the message of the Bible attractive and relevant are also the reasons our students find the Bible uninteresting?

These questions impacted my posture with the guys from this small group. Whether their questions were about their lives or verses in the Bible, or whether they fit in the categories of social justice or personal piety, I did my best to locate their questions on the larger trajectory of their lives. In other words, I was less concerned about rule following and more concerned about giving them an imagination for the kind of people they were and the kind of people they were becoming.

I found that these students would fixate on the specifics of an obscure command or an adult's rigid interpretation of it, which stirred in them a sense of rebellion. But if I could help them zoom out, their curiosity would usually be provoked. In this process, the commands of the Bible became less of an external voice of judgment, and more of an internal voice of invitation for the students to consider who they really were and how these commands could shape who God might be calling them to be.

Years later, this strategy was synthesized into four questions about what the Bible is asking of us and what sort of trajectory our lives are on as followers of Jesus. These were questions our student ministries team would ask adults during their volunteer interviews, that we would talk about with students at coffee shops, that we would sneak into curriculum, and with which we would often end teachings.

The four questions looked something like this:

- What kind of person are you today?

- How is that any different than if you weren't following Jesus? [What kind of person are you today compared to who you used to be?]

- What kind of person is God asking you to become? [What is the trajectory of your story?]

- What role might you play in helping this community become the kind of community God is calling us to be together? [How does the trajectory of your story impact those around you?]

These questions became important companions for us as we read the Bible, and they began to work toward creating a culture among our volunteers and students where we not only took reading the Bible seriously, but also were saying, "We will read and we will obey."

We found that these questions gave a few handles to the mystery of the Gospel: that we are perfectly loved as we are and that we are also on the way to becoming someone new. This transformation has less to do with "trying harder" or "getting all the rules right," and more with having a heart that is willing to say:

I will listen

And

I will obey.

This sort of heart moves us in the right direction on the path of growth, and takes us into another way to read the Bible. It is not just a book to be read; it is a book of commands to be obeyed.

Our students are craving to know that they are invited into something difficult and costly, and therefore worthwhile.

Our students are desperate to know that the Bible is asking something of them and of our church.

TRY THIS ... IN YOUR LIFE:

- Find a journal or some other reflection tool to keep with your Bible. As you read, be more intentional about recording what you're hearing and being asked to obey.

- Ask yourself these four questions:

  - What kind of person are you today?

  - How is that any different than if you weren't following Jesus? [What kind of person are you today compared to who you used to be?]

  - What kind of person is God asking you to become? [What is the trajectory of your story?]

  - What role might you play in helping this community become the kind of community God is calling us to be together? [How does the trajectory of your story impact those around you?]

- Imagine ways that these questions can help you map out your own journey of spiritual growth through engaging Scripture.

- Ask your colleagues, friends, or community what they sense the Bible is currently asking of them.

TRY THIS ... IN YOUR MINISTRY:

- Every time you communicate a rule or expectation to your students, from Scripture or otherwise, offer several clear ways they can experience support from you or other adults to follow the rule or meet the expectation.

- Invite your students to make their Bibles messy. Every time you're reading Scripture and you come across a clear command or exhortation, invite your students to underline or highlight it in their Bible.

- In your conversations with parents or at your next parent meeting, invite them to answer the questions, "What is the Bible asking of your son or daughter in this season of their life?" And maybe even, "What is the Bible asking of you in this season?" Compare their responses to the teachings and curriculum you've been offering your students.

- Instead of creating an application-based teaching or small group curriculum, assign groups to read a large portion of Scripture together. Give them time individually to reflect on the question, "What is this passage asking of me?" and "What is this passage asking of us?" and then invite them to share with the group.

3

A
LAND
TO
EXPERIENCE

IS THE BIBLE AS PHYSICAL AS IT IS SPIRITUAL?

Jesus traveled among all the cities and villages, teaching in their synagogues, announcing the good news of the kingdom, and healing every disease and every sickness.

MATTHEW 9:35

FROM BIBLE SCHOOL TO BIBLE LAND

"I will listen and I will obey" became my mantra for the remainder of my first year of Bible college. Recognizing that God was asking something of me through the Bible was a huge step toward beginning the hard work of orienting my life around what I was reading in Scripture. I thought that once I got my life together, things would start going better for me at Bible school, and it would at the very least begin to feel more like home.

However, just the opposite happened.

The more disciplined I became, and the more I read and studied, the more questions I had. While I felt cared for and supported by my professors and the student life staff at the school, the theological space created there wasn't hospitable to discussion or doubt. The people around me were convinced they knew what God was saying and what God was asking of us. It was my job to be an open receptacle where this information could be deposited. Eventually, my job as a pastor would be to take that deposit and share it with as many other open receptacles as I could find. This was my school's idea of pastoral ministry.

This is how many schools across much of the world do theological education. Our models are based largely on *information transfer.*

While much of the information I was downloading was interesting and helpful, the lack of opportunity for dialogue became increasingly frustrating. Because I hadn't grown up in the church, my questions were often foundational and challenged the assumptions of the instructors or the other students. However, these questions were incredibly important to me because I didn't want to build a house on top of these foundation stones unless it all made sense to me from the bottom up.

I came home for spring break and met with a pastor from my church. I told him that I thought life and the Bible were so much more than what I was experiencing at school, but that if I was wrong, I wasn't sure I wanted to be a Christian anymore. He suggested I go on a mission trip, and invited me to travel to North Africa that summer.

I didn't think people who weren't sure if they wanted to be Christians anymore were ideal candidates for raising support and going on mission trips, but my pastor said that's why he wanted me to go. Then he added that I should leave the "I'm not sure I want to be a Christian anymore" part out of my support letters.

A few months later, I joined four other men from my church on a flight to Spain, where a missionary supported by my church met us and explained how we would spend our two weeks:

We would fill our backpacks with literature and tapes of the Gospels translated into Arabic.

He would drop us off at the border crossing into North Africa and would be back to meet us at the end of our trip.

We were supposed to cross the border and hope no one searched our backpacks, because apparently what we were doing was illegal. This was new information to me.

We received a map of the area and instructions to either hike, hitchhike, or take cabs from town to town.

If we encountered individuals "receptive to the Gospel," we were to give them some of the materials. We would also strategically leave materials in places where an unsuspecting local might discover them.

We had money for hostels, but we also had equipment to sleep outside if necessary.

Finally, the missionary told us not to worry if we were imprisoned—after a few days they would just stamp our passports and send us home.

Yikes.

Despite our lack of cultural training and our concerns about the ethics of this approach, we started out as instructed. We did a lot of hiking, drank a lot of mint tea, and watched a lot of soccer with locals in open-air cafes. And along the way, we did encounter some remarkable people and had some unforgettable spiritual conversations.

One of the surprising gifts of the trip was the companionship we shared on our team. While we were all in different stages of life and asking different questions, we each needed a safe space to dialogue, doubt, and debate. We had a lot of late night conversations about God and the Bible, and the hikes through the rugged desert landscape were filled with laughter, tears, and lively talk.

The leader of our group had been to North Africa and the Middle East before, and he served as an informal guide for many aspects of our experience. One afternoon during the middle of our trip, we were making a long hike between two towns, and the heat from the sun was so intense that it felt like at any moment we would burst into flames. While looking for some shade so we could take a break, we came upon a tree that seemed only slightly bigger than a large bush we might use in landscaping in the US.

As we drank some water and took turns in the shade, the leader of our group asked me to open my hand and hold it out in front of me. I was hesitant, because at this point in our trip we were pulling pranks on each other regularly. Once I finally conceded, he picked something off of one of the branches of the tree and squeezed it open over my hand. Countless black dots fell out, like someone had poured out pepper from a shaker at the kitchen table.

I looked up at him. He said, "Those are mustard seeds. Jesus says that this is all the faith it takes to move a mountain."

I had been reading the Bible and diligently trying to obey it, but I hadn't considered the humanity, geography, and physicality of the text.

In that moment, it felt like time stood still.

Looking back, I think that was the moment I absolutely knew that I wasn't going back to Bible school, because my suspicions about the Bible were proving to be true. The Bible was so much more than I was being taught, and I had to stay on my quest to discover all that it was and is and could be in my life. I had been reading the Bible and diligently trying to obey it, but I hadn't considered the humanity, geography, and physicality of the text. I had never considered that there were *real mustard seeds.* That was the moment I realized the Bible is a book written by real people in real places at real times. It is *real.*

It felt like I had devoted the past three years of my life to studying C.S. Lewis's *Chronicles of Narnia,* yet everyone had forgotten to tell me that Narnia was an actual geographic location on this planet you could go and visit. So, I didn't go back to the same Bible college in the fall, because I didn't want to read about Narnia in the United States, I wanted to learn about Narnia in Narnia, no matter the cost.

And the cost was high.

I had received free tuition at the Bible school I was leaving, and taking on the cost of travel and international schools was a big risk. My parents were supportive, but they were clear with me that I would be footing the bill for this next adventure. This meant working multiple jobs, hustling in every way I could for extra scholarships or cash, and taking out multiple student loans. Many people in my life felt the need to tell me I was crazy. Over and over again.

But if I was going to keep pursuing a relationship with the Bible, I was convinced I needed to feel the same sun that Moses, Ruth, and Jesus felt. I hoped to touch the water of the Jordan River. I imagined hiking the road from Jerusalem to Jericho. I longed to take a boat across the Sea of Galilee. I was desperate to see Jerusalem from the Mount of Olives, and to walk its city streets. At the end of every day, I wanted to wash the same dust off my feet that the Israelites had washed off their feet.

Over the course of several years, I studied in Turkey, Egypt, and Jordan, and lived and studied in Israel twice. The programs I participated in were amazing, and they allowed me to learn from local instructors who opened my eyes to new cultural perspectives on the Bible and the land of Israel. We read our Bibles with compasses and maps, learned about Roman coins and ancient pottery, and dug through excavation reports from biblical sites. We talked with Jewish rabbis and participated in festivals at the synagogue.

The Bible became more than a book to be read and more than a set of rules to be followed.

The Bible became a *land to experience.*

St. Jerome once wrote, "Five Gospels record the life of Jesus. Four you will find in books and the one you will find in the land they call Holy. Read the fifth Gospel and the world of the four will open to you."[1]

I have had the unbelievable privilege of experiencing this "Fifth Gospel" in person. And I recognize this is not a privilege that is available to everyone. I don't necessarily recommend the debt load, either.

But exploring the Middle East taught me that you can experience the "Bible as land" without ever visiting the Holy Land. There are ways you can bring the mentality of

---

1 For more on this, see Bargil Pixner, *With Jesus Through Galilee According to the Fifth Gospel* (Israel: Corazin Publishing, 1992).

such a pilgrimage into your life and into your youth room. This reality has shaped my life and my ministry with young people in three significant ways.

FROM BIBLE LAND TO YOUTH MINISTRY

1. ENCOUNTERING THE PERSON OF JESUS

First, experiencing the Bible as land has changed how I encounter Jesus, and how I talk about Jesus with young people.

When you live in a world where the Bible is primarily a book of rules to be followed, it usually has a dramatic impact on how you view yourself and how you view God. A tenth grader in our ministry once boiled it down like this:

"God is awesome and wants you to be awesome.

You will be awesome if you follow these rules.

You are not awesome.

God is somewhere between heartbroken and really angry about your lack of awesomeness.

God sent his one and only son, Jesus, to follow the rules and be totally awesome on your behalf.

God isn't angry at you anymore.

You don't have to follow the rules anymore, because Jesus already did and you couldn't anyway.

You should try to follow the rules and be awesome out of gratitude to God for sending awesome Jesus.

You are not awesome.

God is awesome.

Repeat." [2]

God's awesomeness, and our lack of awesomeness, prioritizes the need for Jesus to die on the cross for our sins, which is the primary summation of the Gospel many of us communicate in our youth ministries. But this Gospel keeps the Bible at a distance as a set of impossible rules. Similarly, God may be "awesome" but God is kept at a distance, portrayed as vindictive and easily angered. And Jesus is also kept at a distance, forever dead on the cross, bound to the altar as a sacrifice on our behalf, because we will never be awesome enough.

This version of the Gospel isn't untrue, and it's logical, palatable, and especially easy to communicate to young people. But the problem with this Gospel is that it often remains theoretical and Jesus remains disembodied.

As I experienced the Bible connected to land, Jesus moved in my imagination from his sole location on the cross to also

---

2 His ability to be this concise and clear with this content was both remarkable and painful at the same time.

being at the synagogue; from being the sacrifice on the altar to being a teacher on the road and by the sea.

Jesus lived for about thirty-three years before he died. He was a Middle Eastern Jewish rabbi and the son of a carpenter. He had friends and a family, all of whom were marginalized ethnic minorities under the thumb of a tyrannical regime. He had dirt under his fingernails and knew what it meant to be hungry and thirsty. He laughed and he cried. He walked in cities and in the countryside. He was a real person who lived in a real place at a real time. And he had some important things to teach us.

Jesus wasn't a theory. Jesus was and is a person. And you can't make sense of this Jesus and the Bible without situating them in the land and people out of which they were born.

This view of the Bible must also impact the Gospel we share with our students—who are themselves situated in particular social realities in a particular land, reading and interpreting a set of texts originating far away. Far away, but not unimaginably distant.

Therefore, our youth ministry team needed to unravel a few things with our students. We needed to take Jesus off the cross, and let him walk around and teach among us. We needed to try to reconnect all of our proof-texts, curriculum verses, and Bible memory references back into the context and land from which we had removed them. We needed to try to offer a more expansive view of the Gospel that declared that God isn't far away, but has come close, communicating with and through real people at a real place and at a real time. And if God did that "then," God might want to do that now.

This reconnecting work led us to consider a few intentional shifts in what we taught from the scriptures:

From System to Story. We became more aware of the ways we were teaching religious systems and formulas using isolated verses rather than starting with the actual stories of Scripture. Starting with the stories, and trying to teach through the stories, made it much easier to reconnect the Bible to the land out of which it was born. We had to trust that the stories could speak for themselves.

From Savior to Teacher. This shift may be overstated, but it was a necessary pendulum swing for a season. Many of our students knew a formulaic version of the Gospel and Jesus' saving role in it. However, many of them didn't know the actual things Jesus taught during his life and ministry. We spent a significant amount of time and energy trying to help our students imagine a brilliant and creative teacher who said things like, "Look at the birds" in Matthew 6:26 and who also flipped over tables in the crowded outer courts of the Temple (Matthew 21, Mark 11, Luke 19, and John 2). I've found that if you start with Jesus as teacher, the leap to savior comes quite naturally for many people. But it can be possible students will never embrace Jesus as teacher if they start with savior. If you can help young people also see Jesus as teacher, then they will begin to see the land as his classroom.

From Ideas to Incarnation. Our students were desperate to meet a Jesus who made sense of their actual lives and experiences. Much of what they had been taught was connected to trusting in the abstract promises of God or in a spiritual life that had more to do with another world or life after death than the difficult world they inhabited on a daily basis. The Jesus to whom they had been introduced seemed to invite them to escape the flesh-and-blood realities of their actual existence. However, reading the Bible as land reminds us that God is interested in integrating spirit and flesh, not getting us to abandon flesh for spirit. Reading the Bible as land allows us to endure and validate the concrete and messy realities of our students' lives.

2. TEACHING EXPERIENTIALLY

Second, this view of the Bible should not only change what we teach but also how we teach. If the Bible is a land to experience, it has to be more than just information to be explained.

A few years ago, our student ministry team conducted a curriculum evaluation, and we realized that if young people went through all of our programs, from fifth grade to post-high school, they would have had very little exposure to the prophetic books of the Old Testament. This was a problem, as we wanted to help our students engage all parts of the Bible. I energetically volunteered to figure out how to dive more deeply into the prophetic books.

But as I spent some time later that day skimming through the prophets, I regretted the decision. These are not easy books to read, let alone teach to teenagers.

As we worked out a new curriculum over the next year, I remembered my time in Israel, and how the Bible is so earthy and full of word pictures. So, we started our series on the prophets with the story of Ezekiel, who tangibly demonstrates the prophets' deep commitment to God and the Bible. If you're not familiar with the beginning of Ezekiel's story, God tells him to eat a scroll:

"He said to me: Human one, feed your belly and fill your stomach with this scroll that I give you. So I ate it, and in my mouth it became as sweet as honey." (Ezekiel 3:3)

This story taps into an image that appears several times throughout the Bible, that the Word of God is "sweeter than honey." (Psalm 119:103)

Using the lens of the Bible as a book to be read or a set of rules to be followed might lead many of us to craft a teaching compiling several verses about this concept and telling our students how sweet the Bible can be in our lives when we read it and obey it. It would have sounded something like, "Think and read that the LORD is good."

But the Bible as land invites us to say, "Taste and see that the LORD is good" to our students. (Psalm 34:8)

So, I made a giant scroll out of brown craft paper and as I was explaining the beginning of Ezekiel's story, I slowly spread honey all over the scroll, and then about halfway through the talk I started eating the paper with the honey on it. Then, we invited our students and volunteers to taste some fresh honey. Honey is not theoretically sweet. Once you taste it in your mouth, it changes how you feel. You're different because of it. This is the Bible as land.

Here's another example.

A few years ago, I was on a camping trip with students in

the Upper Peninsula of Michigan at the Pictured Rocks National Lakeshore. It is breathtaking.

I had learned the hard way that on experiences like this you have to hold the curriculum loosely, because this is the kind of camping where you sleep in tents and make your food over a fire. There were times when I thought I had the evening "session" planned, but then the pasta took three hours to make, ruining the schedule. (Also, you should never try to make pasta on a camping trip.)

On this particular trip, there was a unique spirit of heaviness among our students. Many of them were going through difficult things at home or school. We had students who were struggling with mental health issues, and several were barely hanging on. Every evening just before lights out I would meet with our leaders, and we would all compare notes on what students shared about their lives during the day:

"I don't have any friends."

"My dad hits me."

"I haven't seen my mom in months."

"My parents are unemployed."

"I was raped."

"I'm struggling with my new meds."

"I tried to kill myself over Christmas break."

Heavy stuff.

As our week together progressed, our leaders shared this overwhelming burden that more than anything, we wanted these students to know how much they were loved by us and by God. This meant chucking the teaching approach we had planned for our hike the next day, and trying to think about how to talk about God's love in a simple, invitational way.

Halfway through our hike we ended up on the beach, where Lake Superior's waves crashed onto the shore. We circled up on the sand, and I simply said,

"Tell me what you know about the love of God."

After a silence, then some quick glances shot like darts by students across our circle as they hoped I wouldn't call on them, a few of the older students shared some ideas. What they shared was good, but it was all information. It was the theoretical love of God. We had a short discussion about what we "know" about the love of God, mostly having to do with Jesus and what Jesus taught us about love.

Then I asked, "What does the love of God *feel* like?"

More silence—only nobody broke it this time.

After allowing the silence to become a bit awkward, I asked,

"Do you want to feel the love of God?"

My sense of confidence in the way I asked the question stirred enough curiosity for many of them to say, "Yes." But their tone sounded more like, "Yes ...?"

I quickly kicked off my hiking boots and asked them to do

the same. I grabbed my Bible and said, "Come with me," and then ran across the beach and into the lake up to my waist. The average temperature of Lake Superior in July is around 60 degrees. The water was cold, and significant waves were crashing into me.

As students reluctantly tiptoed into the water, I asked them not to worry about their clothes or anything else, but to walk in far enough to be able to sit in the water. Once a few of the older students just went for it, the rest followed and sat down. As the brisk water crashed into each of us, sometimes knocking us down or splashing our faces, we screamed and laughed.

Eventually I asked for their attention, and said,

"I know that many of us are carrying a lot right now. And that being here together is good. But we're also constantly reminded of what's waiting for us back home. Hear these words from Psalm 42."

And I read this portion of the text twice:

"Deep calls to deep
    in the roar of your waterfalls;
all your waves and breakers
    have swept over me.

By day the LORD directs his love,
    at night his song is with me—
    a prayer to the God of my life."

(Psalm 42:7-8, NIV)

And then we didn't say anything else. At first there was

more screaming with every wave, then it was laughter, then silence; and finally tears. Some of the students went from sitting in the water to lying down, letting the waves wash over them completely. It was a cathartic and sacred moment.

These students who had read their Bibles and knew information and verses about the love of God were actually *feeling* it, and it was transforming and healing them.

I think many of the students would have remained there all day if we had let them. But we had five more miles to hike, and we had to make it back to camp before dark. The hike from the beach was radically different than the hike to the beach. The heaviness we had felt seemed so much lighter. There was a sense of joy among our group.

At the campfire that night, one student said, "That was the coolest thing I've ever experienced."

She encountered the love of God in a transformative way, because she experienced the Bible as land.

I don't know why ideas like eating a piece of paper drenched in honey or sitting in water together didn't come to me more easily, because they're no different than someone asking me to hold out my hand and spilling mustard seeds of faith into it. Reading the Bible as land and inviting your students to do the same means less explanation and more experience. It means saying, "Open your hand, taste this honey, feel these waves, come follow me, close your eyes, imagine if, drink this, touch that, and look over there."

What might your teaching look like if you invited your

students and volunteers into this sort of experience with the Bible on a more regular basis?

DISCOVERING WORD PICTURES

One of the primary ways biblical writers communicate their message is by using word pictures and experiential imagery that are connected to the lands of the Middle East and North Africa in which they lived. One practice I've committed to is making a note in the back of my Bible every time I come across one of these images. If you try this, it won't be long before you run out of space to write down everything you're discovering. Here are a few word pictures I and others have drawn from to engage students experientially:

But I have calmed and quieted myself, like a weaned child on its mother; I'm like the weaned child that is with me. (Psalm 131:2)

I am the vine; you are the branches. If you remain in me and I in you, then you will produce much fruit. Without me, you can't do anything. (John 15:5)

How terrible it will be for you legal experts and Pharisees! Hypocrites! You are like whitewashed tombs. They look beautiful on the outside. But inside they are full of dead bones and all kinds of filth. In the same way you look righteous to people. But inside you are full of pretense and rebellion. (Matthew 23:27-28)

Your word is a lamp before my feet and a light for my journey. (Psalm 119:105)

Like birds flying aloft, so the LORD of heavenly forces will shield Jerusalem: shielding and saving, sparing and rescuing. (Isaiah 31:5)

On the last and most important day of the festival, Jesus stood up and shouted, "All who are thirsty should come to me! All who believe in me should drink! As the scriptures said concerning me, Rivers of living water will flow out from within him." (John 7:37-38)

God's Spirit blows wherever it wishes. You hear its sound, but you don't know where it comes from or where it is going. It's the same with everyone who is born of the Spirit. (John 3:8)

The LORD is my shepherd. I lack nothing. (Psalm 23:1)

Then the angel showed me the river of life-giving water, shining like crystal, flowing from the throne of God and the Lamb through the middle of the city's main street. On each side of the river is the tree of life, which produces twelve crops of fruit, bearing its fruit each month. The tree's leaves are for the healing of the nations. (Revelation 22:1-3)

3. READING LESS BIBLE

Finally, I realized I needed to start learning more about the Bible by reading it a little less.

If we're going to experience the Bible as land, in Israel or at home, and invite others to come with us, we need to continue to learn as much as we can about the world out of which the Bible was born. If it is a book written by real people in real places during real times, we need to become more familiar with those people, places, and times. This likely means reading the Bible a little less when we are preparing to teach, and saving some time for other books, conversations, and online searches about maps, roads, coins, excavation reports, Roman culture, pagan religion, city life, and Second Temple Judaism.

Reading the Bible less can help us discover what a simple word like "up" means. One summer we were doing a series on the Gospels for our students, and every week we referred to the same maps of Israel for a better idea of what

Jesus and his disciples were doing. After several weeks, we were talking through one of the stories where Jesus went "up" to Jerusalem and one of our students interrupted, asking, "The verse we just read said Jesus went 'up,' but on the map, it looks like he went 'down' to Jerusalem from Galilee. How come it says 'up' and not 'down'?" (See Matthew 20:17.)

I knew exactly where this question was coming from. Having grown up in an area where "up" means north and "down" means south, this student thought the text was saying Jesus went "north" from Galilee to Jerusalem, when Jerusalem is actually south of Galilee.

I asked the group for their thoughts, and a few interesting theories emerged about hemispheres, magnetic fields, and whether compasses work in the Middle East. Then I put the map back on our projection screen and we talked for a few minutes about topography. I know—sounds exciting, doesn't it? But it actually was.

I explained that Jerusalem and the temple were built on top of a mountain, like most ancient cities, and that a trip to Jerusalem from just about any place in Israel was an uphill hike. Jesus was walking "up" a mountain every time he went to Jerusalem.

The student who asked this question then said, "So he was probably pretty tired when he got there. Wow, he was tired a lot. I guess I've never thought about Jesus being tired."

In a moment of brilliance, one of our leaders asked, "Have you ever been really tired? Jesus has, too."

Without flying on a plane and traveling to Israel, and without even leaving our church building, the land out of which the Bible was born spoke to us in a transformative way. If you want to get technical, the topography of Israel was instrumental in helping high school students understand and be transformed by the incarnation of Christ.

Reading the Bible as land can reveal the countless ways that the world of the Bible differs from our own, and it can also reveal striking similarities. Discovering that the Jewish people of the first century were a marginalized and oppressed nation, under religious persecution at the hands of the most powerful global superpower at the time, can cause us to reinterpret and rethink many of our own interpretations and theological concepts, especially if they were constructed from positions of power and privilege.

For many of us, this can cause us to become more aware of the systems we participate in and the ways we may be perpetuating a modern-day "Roman" culture. For others of us, it can provide a deep sense of solidarity through the Incarnation; that our God comes to us as the poorest of the poor in an oppressive location and situation. This situation is an experience that many of us may be familiar with, or it may be deeply unfamiliar, or both experiences may exist in the same youth group. This is why considering how we read the Bible is so important. When we

When we become more aware of how we read the Bible, we discover the "we" is much bigger and more diverse than we ever knew.

become more aware of how we read it, we discover the "we" is much bigger and more diverse than we ever knew.

Youth workers constantly face the temptation of allowing the world of our teenagers to shape how we teach the Bible. We so desperately want to be relevant that we actually strip away the power of the Bible with our method, and the Gospel becomes far less compelling.

While Roman coins and ancient roads seem less interesting than the latest band or teen craze, my experience tells me that our young people crave an invitation into a world different from their own, and that if we invite them into an adventure in this land, the Bible will become so much more than it has ever been.

TRY THIS ... IN YOUR LIFE:

- Ask your senior pastor or a colleague to share a resource with you that has expanded their understanding of the world of the Bible.

- Commit thirty to sixty minutes each week learning "about the Bible" from an outside source (Googling, archeological journals, atlases, podcasts, videos, etc.). A few recommendations include:

    - Be the only youth worker in town with a subscription to *Biblical Archaeology Review*, an accessible, scholarly journal.

- Check out the work of Ray VanderLaan and *That the World May Know Ministries* for videos and articles on Jesus and the land of Israel.

- If you want to place stories of the Bible on maps as you read, take a look at the workbook-style resource *Regions on the Run: Introductory Map Studies in the Land of the Bible*, by James M. Monson.

- Anything you would normally do inside that you could also do outside, do outside, just to experience the land around you. Do this whether you live in a broad countryside or the heart of a crowded city.

- Find an (affordable) outdoor retreat or pilgrimage experience, and go for your own formation.

- As you read the Bible, take note of any nature-based and city-based images or word pictures. Reflect on your notes as often as possible, being mindful of how they impact what you experience each day.

- Spend time reflecting on whether the Gospel you believe is primarily focused on the death of Jesus or the life of Jesus, and how the differences between these two aspects of the Gospel have impacted your life.

TRY THIS ... IN YOUR MINISTRY:

- Experiment with word pictures and images from the Bible and how you might introduce them to your students in an experiential way.

- Anything you would normally do inside that you can also do outside, do outside. This will look different depending on the location of your church, and that's okay. Maximize your opportunities to experience earthy fields or city streets, cemeteries or hilltop parks, to tangibly encounter the text.

- Whenever the text you're teaching includes geographic locations, include a map in your presentation (or show students how to look at the maps inevitably waiting in the backs of their Bibles) and explain the significance of that location as part of your teaching.

- Focus on one particular biblical passage or story for a season. Invite students and leaders to group together and focus on varying aspects of the story—words, culture, geography, time period—and have each group share how their specific feature uniquely influences the story.

- Ask students and leaders to share about a time when they felt they "experienced" the Bible in a physical way.

4

A
WAY
TO
LIVE

ARE WE LIVING THE BEST KIND OF LIFE TODAY?

The thief enters only to steal, kill, and destroy. I came so that they could have life—indeed, so that they could live life to the fullest.

JOHN 10:10

[IM]PERSONAL EVANGELISM

One of the courses I was required to take during my first semester of Bible college was a class called "Personal Evangelism." The point of the course was to equip students with ways to share the Gospel effectively with others, and invite them to convert to Christianity. We read books by brilliant missiologists and pastors, talked about how to be persuasive with our words, and had to memorize relevant Bible passages. The class culminated in a final project where we wrote a paper detailing our experience going to the busy shopping district downtown and "witnessing to" ten strangers, using the methods we had learned to share about Jesus as the way to salvation.

On a cold Friday afternoon in December, I walked downtown just a few hours before my paper was due, without having "witnessed to" anyone yet. I didn't expect that finding ten strangers to talk to would be a problem.

I also didn't expect to see the rest of my forty classmates on the same two city blocks, trying to meet the requirements of our assignment, while also trying to save people from hell. We had all procrastinated, and the clock was ticking.

Heaven, hell, and final first semester grades were all at stake.

Regardless of the mixed motives, I think it's worth celebrating that four hundred people heard some form of the Gospel that day, even if it was from cold, nervous, and stammering college students reciting memorized

Bible verses. I wish I could share stories of repentance, conversion, and revival because of the forty passionate students desperately sharing their faith with so many complete strangers that day. The most unfortunate part of this assignment was that there is no way to know whether or not these conversations made a long-term difference in anyone's life. That's true of a lot of things we do in ministry, but feels especially pertinent in retrospect on this exercise.

While most of my conversations involved getting yelled at, people asking me questions that my training didn't prepare me for, and a fair amount of embarrassment on my part, I know for certain that God did change at least one life through that experience.

Mine.

I left the shopping district that afternoon with just enough material to write a decent paper, along with a good amount of shame, doubt, and questions about what on earth it meant to be a Christian. I really wanted to get my paper done, but also share the Good News and help these people find Jesus. But I was disillusioned, wondering if I was actually just an annoying obstacle to people finding the perfect gift to put under the Christmas tree.

One of the Bible verses we were required to memorize in preparation for this assignment was John 14:6, when Jesus says, "I am the way, the truth, and the life." We were trained to lead with other passages of Scripture in our conversations, and this passage was the secret tool to have the edge in any conversation. This was the "power verse" we used to make sure people understood that eternity was at stake. If Jesus is "the way," then Jesus is the only way to heaven.

In basketball terms, asking people if they knew where they would go when they died was the alley-oop, and John 14:6 was the slam dunk.

But that afternoon I realized this sort of evangelistic method had reduced the Gospel—the best news the universe has ever heard—to fire insurance, and I wasn't a very good insurance salesman. I wasn't able to answer some very basic questions that people asked in response to my prepared presentation. The few people who allowed me to disrupt their shopping had questions about war and poverty, love and relationships, and politics and peace. In short, my presentation was about making sure people had considered the afterlife, while they had deep and desperate questions about their actual lives now. These people weren't interested in a God who didn't seem interested in this world and this life, and I was discovering that I wasn't either.

> *These people weren't interested in a God who didn't seem interested in this world and this life, and I was discovering that I wasn't either.*

I wasn't an effective salesman that day, partly because I wasn't sure I could buy what I was selling.

Back in the safety of my dorm room, two of my observations in my reflection paper (as I raced against the clock to meet my deadline) were that there had to be a better way to share the Good News with people, and that the Good News had to be better news than the news I was sharing.

SHOW ME THE WAY

That sink-or-swim experience in personal evangelism is one of the factors that eventually led me to study in Israel. My beliefs about the Bible were changing, but I didn't know what to replace those beliefs with. I didn't even have a new set of questions to replace the questions I had been handed. As it turned out, the person who helped transform my understanding of Christianity and the Bible during this time period was a Jewish rabbi.

During my first season of studying in Israel, I took a course called "Jewish Thought and Practice" taught by a rabbi. He was born in the United States, but had lived in Israel most of his life. He was raised in an Orthodox home and taught at a Conservative school, but participated in a Reform synagogue.[1] His course was basically "Judaism for Christians 101." He walked us through biblical and modern Jewish holidays, synagogue practices, and how Judaism relates to Islam and Christianity. It was one of the best classes I've ever taken.

What intrigued me most about the instructor was how much he knew about Jesus. He would often mention one of Jesus' teachings or a Christian belief as a way of relating to our class of Christian students in a "We have one of

---

1 Without getting too technical, all this really means is that he's experienced the full spectrum of modern Judaism.

those too" sort of way. And sometimes he would mention the teachings of Jesus to offer new insight from a Jewish perspective in a "You've heard it said, but I tell you" sort of way.[2] In fact, he knew the New Testament better than any of us. This opened up all sorts of interesting questions and conversations about Judaism, Christianity, and Jesus.

The rabbi's teaching would often put my classmates and me in a strange position. My professor was the type of person I was supposed to approach during my evangelism project to talk about Jesus as "the way." He knew the New Testament better than any Christian I had ever met, and had so much interesting insight on Jesus, but I wondered what he actually thought about the concept of Jesus as the only way to heaven. While I was stepping away from that sort of evangelism and use of the Bible, I didn't yet know what I was stepping toward.

One day I stayed after class to ask some questions. I casually inquired about the day's lecture content, and then finally dropped the question I spent most of our class period working up the courage to ask:

"What did Jesus mean in John 14 when he said he was 'the way,' and do you think he was talking about heaven, and do you think Jesus is the only way to heaven?"

It was really three questions nervously smashed into one awkward inquiry. The look he gave me was a mix of annoyance and compassion. He was used to dealing with us evangelicals who couldn't learn from him without

---

2 This is one of Jesus' great teaching techniques in what's commonly known as the Sermon on the Mount in Matthew chapters 5-7. See Matthew 5:21-22, 27-28, 31-32, 33-34, 38-39, 43-44.

also trying to convert him. He responded, "I don't believe Jesus is the only way to heaven because as a Jew I'm not concerned about the afterlife. The Bible doesn't really talk about the afterlife. I don't think this is what Jesus was talking about. I think Jesus was talking about 'way' in the same manner all of the other rabbis did from that time period. He's talking about 'the way you walk.'"

His response brought me a simultaneous sense of relief and intensity. The rabbi wasn't nearly as emotionally connected to my question as I was, which calmed my nerves, yet his response cut to the heart of who Jesus was and what he came to teach us, which carried with it a deep sense of urgency. He didn't offer the clarity I was looking for, and I didn't understand what he meant enough to know if I agreed with him. However, the rabbi provided me sufficient insight to persist with my hunch that that there was more to this passage than a modern evangelistic method, and that I needed to keep pursuing a better way.

A BETTER WAY

Most people I know are desperately looking for a better way of life in a world that feels increasingly complex. Many of us feel like we're barely getting by with the basic demands of work and relationships, let alone the constant stream of updates about terrorism, globalism, pluralism, racism, tribalism, economic collapse, food scarcity, global warming, war, and genocide that fill our (and our students') newsfeeds. Of course, these realities are much more visceral than our newsfeeds, and some of us may experience their personal impact daily.

We're looking for a faith that does more than get us from this life to the next, one that validates and actually "works" in our current lives. Young people are not just wondering "Is it true?" they are also wondering, "Does it work?"

We're looking for a better way.

And so are our young people.

According to research conducted by the Fuller Youth Institute for the Growing Young project, churches that are effective in engaging young people are talking differently when they talk about Jesus. When FYI reviewed hundreds of hours of interview transcripts, they found that churches growing young are taking Jesus' message seriously in three key ways:

1. There is less talk about abstract beliefs and more talk about Jesus as a person.

2. Faith is less tied to formulas and more focused on a redemptive narrative.

3. There is less emphasis on heaven later and more on life here and now.

A church leader who was interviewed as part of this research project stated, "The Gospel is not a moment or transaction; it is not even simply a message; it is actually a *new way of living*, a new reality that is intended to pervade everything in this life, and it has both present and eternal implications."[3]

---

3 Kara Powell, Jake Mulder, and Brad Griffin, *Growing Young: 6 Essential Strategies to Help Young People Discover and Love Your Church* (Grand Rapids: Baker, 2016), 136-141. See fulleryouthinstitute.org/growingyoung.

Can the Bible be more than "Basic Instructions Before Leaving Earth" (a handy acrostic you may have heard to define the Bible's significance), despite the convenience of this catchy phrasing?

Can we discover a faith for our own lives and for our young people that matters in this life too?

Maybe the rabbi was right. Is there a better way?

THE WAY OF JESUS

Throughout the Hebrew Bible, or Old Testament, the writers give a vision of what the "way of God" or the "way of the righteous" looks like, often in contrast to the "way of the wicked":

> "Listen ... then the years of your life will be many.
> I teach you the path of wisdom.
> I lead you in straight courses.
> When you walk, you won't be hindered;
> when you run, you won't stumble.
> Hold on to instruction; don't slack off;
> protect it, for it is your life.
> Don't go on the way of the wicked;
> don't walk on the path of evil people.
> Avoid it! Don't turn onto it;
> stay off of it and keep going!"
> (Proverbs 4:10-15)

> "God! His way is perfect;
> the LORD's word is tried and true.
> He is a shield for all who take refuge in him."
> (Psalm 18:30)

> "I will think about your precepts
> and examine all your paths."
> (Psalm 119:15)

> "I've chosen the way of faithfulness;
> I'm set on your rules."
> (Psalm 119:30)

In the Hebrew Bible, "the way" became synonymous with "Law" or "Torah," often in contrast to another way. It's as if God is consistently saying, "There's my way and then there's another way. There's righteousness and then there's wickedness. There's law and then there's lawlessness. There's my wisdom and then there's the wisdom of the world. Which will you choose?" In fact, this understanding of "way" wasn't exclusive to the Bible. It was a common ancient metaphor for the active participation in religious beliefs, teachings, or practices.

As the story of the Jewish people unfolded, understanding of "the way" progressed from being more than just the Torah, to being how you put the Torah into practice. The image that became associated with "way" was that of a path. It was the way you walked and the way you followed the Torah's commands. And, as always, there is no shortage of paths you can take with your life. There's living faithfully and staying on God's path, and then there's going another way.

There's living faithfully and staying on God's path, and then there's going another way.

As you can imagine, opinions varied widely on what this "way" was supposed to look like. As I mentioned in Chapter 2, there were all kinds of debates on what it looked like to live out this way among the Jewish people of the first century. These arguments were heated because they were ultimately about faithfulness and discerning how God would have them live their lives.

After all, none of us want to end up accidentally walking down the path of the wicked or living out the way of folly. Mix in a few political agendas and struggles for power between the Pharisees, Sadducees, Essenes, and Zealots, as well as differing perspectives associated with various regions of Israel, and you have a recipe for all sorts of different interpretations and prescriptions about "the way" people should live. It's not hard for us to imagine a world that includes heated religious debates tinged with political affiliations, regional conflict, and the desire for power, since this is the landscape that many find themselves in today.

These are the circumstances and the types of conversations happening when Jesus arrives on the scene and says:

"Do not think that I have come to abolish the Law or the Prophets; I have not come to abolish them but to fulfill them." (Matthew 5:17, NIV)

Jesus dives into the theological and spiritual debates of his time, saying he came to "fulfill" the Torah, or to show us what "the way" truly looks like.

Jesus didn't come to "abolish" a way of life.

Jesus came to "fulfill," or "show us," this way of life.

What Jesus is saying here is really important if we're going to get to the true heart of his life and message. In my experience, Christians sometimes confuse the words "abolish" and "fulfill" and therefore miss out on the meaning of "way." The line of thinking often looks like this:

Jesus didn't come to abolish, or get rid of, the way.

"Fulfill" means that Jesus perfectly lived out the way.

So now we don't have to live out the way, because Jesus did it for us.

Jesus "fulfilling the way" essentially means "abolishing the way" in our lives.

So, Jesus came to fulfill the way so we could get rid of the way.

See the issue with this approach to understanding Jesus and the way? It becomes even more problematic when we read the verses that follow this passage. Jesus begins the Sermon on the Mount in Matthew 5 with this affirmation of the Law and the Prophets, saying he's not interested in getting rid of them, but in fulfilling them. He then goes on to offer a radical reinterpretation and retelling of significant parts of the Torah. It's like Jesus is saying, "This is what the way is supposed to look like!"

If we read John 14:6 in this context, when Jesus says, "I am the way," he is making a claim even more radical than being the exclusive portal to the afterlife. He is claiming to be "the way personified," the incarnation of "the way."

Jesus is saying that he is the way *interpreted*.

Jesus is saying that he is the way in *action*.

Jesus is saying, "If you want to know what it looks like to live this thing out, look at me!"

I think the early followers of Jesus had some grasp of this radical claim. In several places in the book of Acts, the first Christians (before they were called Christians) were referred to as "followers of the way," because they were committed to living out Jesus' way together.[4]

It wasn't about a set of beliefs.

It wasn't about being a part of a country club or social group.

It wasn't only about life after death or eternal security.

It wasn't about keeping commandments.

It wasn't about making one specific decision.

It was about living a certain way right now.

It was centering their lives and communities around the

---

4 Acts 9:2, 19:9, 19:23, 22:4, 24:14, 24:22

radical claim that the way of Jesus was the best possible way to live. It is the life God made us to live.[5]

For those early followers, living out Jesus' way was what it meant to be a Christian.

And the same invitation is extended to us.

It's an invitation young people around us are searching for. It's good news. Dallas Willard put it this way:

> As a disciple of Jesus I am with him, by choice and by grace, learning from him how to live in the Kingdom of God … I am learning from Jesus to live my life as he would live my life if he were I. I am not necessarily learning to do everything he did, but I am learning how to do everything I do in the manner that he did all that he did.[6]

In *The Very Good Gospel*, Lisa Sharon Harper tells a story about asking a group of campus ministry leaders, "What is the gospel?" during a training workshop. Despite all of the formulas and answers they had learned, a void emerged at the core of their message. Harper divided the group into four teams to explore each Gospel writer's version of the Good News and bring their findings back to the group. They discovered connections they had not seen before. Harper writes,

> The team members found that Matthew,

---

5 The mission of the student ministry I helped lead for a number of years was, "Helping Students Live the Best Kind of Life—The Life God Made Us to Live".

6 Dallas Willard, *The Divine Conspiracy: Rediscovering Our Hidden Life in God* (New York: HarperCollins, 1997), 283.

Mark, Luke, and John all cared about an individual's reconciliation with God, self, and their communities. But the Gospel writers also focused on systemic justice, peace between people groups, and freedom for the oppressed. The good news was both about the *coming* of the Kingdom of God and the *character* of that Kingdom. It was about what God's Kingdom looked like ... The biblical Gospel writers' good news was about the restoration of shalom.[7]

The Good News of the Kingdom of God is a vision of a new way to live. Not only forever, but also right now.

SHOW THEM THE WAY

How could this view of Jesus and the Bible shape the way we care for our young people?

Perhaps we need to move from burden to invitation.

We have to consider a fundamental redefinition of how we view what the Bible might be trying to accomplish. My experience tells me that much of Christian tradition and much of our Christian interpretation of Jewish tradition views the law and Torah as a burden, because trying to do the things prescribed in the Hebrew Bible is an impossible task no one has ever been able to accomplish. In this scenario, the main purpose the law serves is to show

7 Lisa Sharon Harper, *The Very Good Gospel: How Everything Wrong Can Be Made Right* (New York: WaterBrook, 2016), 6.

us and to show God how sinful and incapable we are as human beings. This limited view of the law also limits our view of Jesus, because it reduces him into the mechanism by which we are rescued from having to keep the law.

But Jesus' definition, or redefinition, of the law crashes directly into this limited view. Jesus condemns religious leaders who burden individuals with the law and claims that his burden is light (Matthew 11:30). Because when you walk on his path, you experience life. Jesus claims the law as life and himself as the personification of it. Jesus affirms the law as the "way" and invites everyone to join him on that path.

"Come to me, all you who are struggling hard and carrying heavy loads, and I will give you rest. Put on my yoke, and learn from me. I'm gentle and humble. And you will find rest for yourselves. My yoke is easy to bear, and my burden is light."

MATTHEW 11:28-30

Reading the Bible as "way" reveals why reading it as "rules" is merely one location on a much larger map when it comes to how we read the Bible. Law implies burden, but way implies invitation. Reading the Bible as "way" helps us to see that God isn't waiting to zap us for screwing up; instead, God is interested in inviting us into the fullest, most

Law implies burden, but way implies invitation.

beautiful life—the one for which he created us in the first place.

Here's what this can look like in your conversations, relationships, and teachings with young people:

1. ACKNOWLEDGE THAT THERE ARE SO MANY WAYS WE CAN LIVE OUR LIVES.

Name the brokenness, pain, and sorrow that many of our young people experience on a daily basis because of the way that they or others choose to live. This is important because, first, it demonstrates empathy and understanding on your part as their leader. This is incarnational ministry at its best, and it's a significant part of how Jesus lived out the way. Additionally, this is important because the reality of your students' actual lives will nearly always cause them to experience dissonance when you talk about the way of Jesus. Until students have some sense that you can comprehend what their lives are like, it will be difficult for them to respond to your call to another way. Starting with acknowledging will also help you know if your message is overly focused on the afterlife at the expense of taking their current lives seriously.

2. SHOW THEM EXAMPLES OF THE FRUIT OF THIS NEW WAY OF LIVING.

Perhaps many of our youth ministries have mastered the art of "telling" people about Jesus, but I wonder how much we're missing the mark when it comes to "showing" people what living out the way of Jesus looks like? Without becoming prescriptive, introduce people, stories, and images of what it looks like when someone lives out "the way" in their own context. Some of these examples can come from the Bible. In addition, show them a diversity of friendships, relationships, marriages, careers, college choices, justice initiatives, personal integrity, sacrifices, and risky decisions that put the way of Jesus on display today.

Ideally, some of these examples would come from your own life and from the lives of people who are much different than you and others in your context. Show them that another way is beautiful and possible, and not too difficult for them or beyond their reach (see Deuteronomy 30:11). This way involves the transformation of the Spirit in their lives. I want to be clear that I'm not advocating that we "show" and don't "tell," but that we try to move the pendulum back into balance in our youth ministries between these two realities. The life and ministry of Jesus display how to hold both in tension.

In our youth ministry, this was as simple as inviting specific students and leaders who were compellingly putting the way of Jesus on display in a specific area of their lives to share a brief testimony during our weekly gatherings. On a larger level, as a team we decided to take this further by dedicating a time every spring to sharing stories of people throughout history who were showing us something unique with the way they lived their lives. For example, rather than doing a Bible study together, we watched short films about Dr. Martin Luther King, Jr., Elizabeth Elliot, Brother

Yun, Mother Teresa, and Saint Francis, and then wondered together what their lives could uniquely show us about the way of life that Jesus was calling each of us to consider.

3. IMAGINE WITH STUDENTS THAT THERE MIGHT BE ANOTHER WAY, A BETTER WAY, OR EVEN A BEST WAY.

I would even recommend staying away from "right" or "wrong" language, but begin sentences with phrases like:

"What if …?"

"Have you ever considered …?"

"How about …?"

"Can you imagine if …?"

"What if we tried …?"

When we invite young people to consider another way, we can begin to cultivate an individual and collective imagination for what life could be like. This sort of imagination can lead to all sorts of redemptive possibilities, and all sorts of "ways" for students to live out "the way." Then your role is to support your students as they work to make their imagined reality possible in their lives, and to name and celebrate the work of God in and through them.

I get a nervous stomach when I think about returning to that downtown shopping district to participate in street evangelism. But if I did return, I would have confidence in inviting people to consider something more than only life after death.

Because Jesus says, "I am the way."

And he invites, "Come, follow me."

I would love to invite them into the biggest, fullest, most beautiful way of life possible: the way of Jesus. The life we were made for. I didn't realize it then, but this is what I was searching for, and I think they might have been as well.

LIVING IN THE TENSION AS WE READ THE BIBLE

I'm hoping that by now you're asking some questions about how each chapter of this book intersects with the others. Specifically, reading the Bible as "the way" or "the life God made us to live" offers a contrast to Chapter 2, which emphasized reading the Bible as commands and considering what Scripture might be asking of us. The tension you may feel between these two chapters is a tension that is found within the actual scriptures. Just like in our modern world, the ancient writers had differing perspectives on God and what it means to live in relationship to God. I have shown you passages from the

Bible that seem to indicate that obedience to God is the motivation for considering the commands found in the Bible, while other passages of Scripture seem to indicate that the Bible is inviting us into a different way of life, as much for our own good as it is for obeying God. Sometimes this difference may be mostly rhetorical. I imagine there have been times you have been more confrontational with your students ("Do this!" or "Stop doing that!") because of the urgency of a situation or a passion from which you were speaking, and other times you've been more gentle and imaginative in your approach. We see this sort of pastoral nuance in the Bible as well.

So, what do we do with this tension? I would invite you to consider resisting the temptation to resolve the tension right way, but to allow these multiple perspectives and images to challenge your assumptions or beliefs about approaching the Bible. Many of us leap to dismiss or dismantle one side of a conversation and elevate another. This is natural. However, this quick dismissal can limit our ability to have an expanding experience of the Bible and the diversity of ways that the church globally has engaged and currently engages these texts.

Living in this tension can be difficult, especially if you're doing it alone. I'd highly recommend finding a conversation partner or small group of people you can process these ideas with. Engaging the tension with other people, resisting the temptation to quickly resolve it, and practicing the ability to balance multiple perspectives can be a sign of a growing and maturing faith.

TRY THIS ... IN YOUR LIFE:

- Consider the questions, "What way are you living?" and "How does this way reflect the way of Jesus?"

- Ask friends, family members, and colleagues to reflect back to you by responding to the question, "What kind of life am I putting on display?"

- Focus on reading the Gospels in your own devotional life, responding to the statement, "Jesus is inviting me to [blank]" after every passage you read.

- Acknowledge someone in your own life who is "showing you" what the way of Jesus looks like, and ask them to mentor you or become more intentional about spending time with you.

TRY THIS ... IN YOUR MINISTRY:

- Spend some time with your volunteers trying to gauge whether or not they feel they're experiencing the way of Jesus as the best possible way to live, and identify what obstacles or barriers they're encountering while trying to experience this life.

- Ask students and leaders how being a Christian has impacted both their present life and their future life.

- Lead a study on the life and teachings of Jesus, making note of how often Jesus talks about the afterlife, and how much Jesus talks about life here and now. Highlight themes of what Jesus talks about most.

- Give your students a survey to collect as much information as possible about what they're experiencing in their life on a daily basis. Ask questions like, "What is the most difficult part of your day?" and, "Who in your life most impacts your choices?" Collect all the joy, sorrow, and pain anonymously, and consider how it might inform your team's work with young people to help them experience the Gospel.

- With your students, create an evangelism approach that highlights why following Jesus is the best possible way to live. Help them practice how to share the Gospel through the new words and practices they imagine.

- Create some space in your programming on a semi-regular basis to acknowledge students or volunteers who are uniquely "showing you" what the way of Jesus looks like by the way they're living their lives.

5

A
STORY
TO
ENGAGE

WHAT DOES THE BIBLE TELL US ABOUT THE WORLD AND OUR PLACE IN IT?

Heaven is declaring God's glory;
the sky is proclaiming his handiwork.
One day gushes the news to the next,
and one night informs another what needs to be known.
Of course, there's no speech, no words—
their voices can't be heard—
but their sound extends throughout the world;
their words reach the ends of the earth.

PSALM 19:1-4

THE BIG WORLD

Michigan's Upper Peninsula is one of my favorite places in the world. It feels like sacred ground for so many reasons. And as I mentioned in chapter 3, for a number of years, I spent a week each summer camping and hiking with high school students at the Pictured Rocks National Lakeshore on Lake Superior.

We would cook together, go on ten-mile hikes, and spend the evenings around campfires. When we first started taking students camping, I was surprised by how many of them had never experienced nature in many ways I had taken for granted. Many had never been camping, slept outside, made their own food, or watched a sunrise. Regardless of the packing list and instructions we provided ahead of time, their newbie status was always demonstrated by the number of students who only packed skinny jeans for a week of camping and hiking.

One of the many goals we had for trips like this was to expose teenagers to the beauty of our world, even if it was something as simple as watching a sunset together. I was willing to go to great lengths to make this happen, even if it meant a large amount of silliness and a small amount of deception.

It was always our goal to get to the beach before dark, after dinner and cleanup. Enjoying the beach at dusk with a group of high school students after a day of hiking meant a lot of screaming, swimming, splashing, football, and everyone running in different directions. While I thoroughly enjoyed this time, my primary goal was actually to watch the sunset together.

During the chaos of our evening time at the beach, I would ask students to come into the water with me, usually pretty far out from shore, but close enough that we could still touch the bottom. The lake's water is always cold, and as the sun was setting it would get even colder. I would ask everyone to form a line together and to face the setting sun.

This is where the silliness comes in. I would ask everyone to take a few deep breaths because I wanted to share with them one of the great mysteries of the universe. What I would share went something like this:

"If you're in the water when the sun is setting, at the exact moment when the sun hits the water, you can actually feel the water getting warmer. The sun is millions of degrees, and Lake Superior is cold. When you put something that hot in such cold water, you will feel it get warmer. Isn't it amazing that the sun is so hot that when it hits the water, it can warm up a lake as large as Lake Superior?"

This is likely just one of the many false teachings I've intentionally or unintentionally offered to my students. And, I know, it's totally absurd. But there would always be a few students, and some leaders, who would turn their head sideways toward me and ask, "Really?"

And I'd say, "Pay attention, let's see if we can feel it."

Others would smirk, wink, and play along.

For those of us who were willing to put down the football or stop running around, there we would stand. Sometimes there would only be a handful of us, sometimes there would be thirty of us, all taking in a sunset in silence.

What was actually happening in this moment? Perhaps we were being silly. But it was the best way I knew to invite students to be present. We were present to ourselves and present to the world around us for just a few minutes. For some of our students and leaders, it was for the first time in their lives.

There were always a few people who would claim they felt the water get warmer, and that may have been for other reasons.[1] But when the sun set, and someone eventually broke the silence, they made comments like:

"That was beautiful."

"That was awesome."

"That's one of the most amazing things I've ever seen."

This moment always inspired awe and wonder. Our swim back to the beach carried the weight of reverence. It was like these teenagers, in the sight of something so remarkable, couldn't help but be more reserved. They were silenced by the splendor of nature.

Later, around a campfire or in our tents, we would have the most meaningful conversations of the day. Students——and some adult volunteers——would admit and wonder aloud:

"I don't know what I'm supposed to do with my life."

And

---

1 I don't need to tell you why.

"I think I need to make some changes."

And

"It seems like there is more to the world than what we can see."

And

"Where did all of this come from?"

And

"Who made this?"

For most of us, these types of moments don't happen every day. Some of us only experience them a few times in our lives while looking up at the stars, scaling a mountain, immersed in a massive city crowd, caught in a blizzard, experiencing the birth of a child, or praying in silence and stillness. These moments reinforce that so much of life is a mystery, and that our lives are somehow both infinitely large and indescribably small. We're overwhelmed with wonder and awe, and something is provoked within us, causing us to ask the big questions of life.

THE BIG STORY

I don't think it's an accident that God's early redemptive work on earth involves a similar situation. God reaches out to a human family, Abram and Sarai, in Genesis 12.

A few chapters later in Genesis 15, God wants to formalize this agreement. God tells Abram:

"I am your shield, your very great reward."

And then at dusk God leads Abram outside and tells him to look at the stars, and tells him:

"So shall your offspring be."

The author of the book of Hebrews reflects that from this one elderly man and woman, "as good as dead, came descendants as numerous as the stars in the sky and as countless as the sand on the seashore." (Hebrews 11:12, NIV)

There is an important lesson hidden in this story: God's redemptive work in the world involves gazing at the stars and the sand, and receiving a greater vision for who we are and who God is.

And that's also another aspect of what the Bible is for us. The Bible is meant to be read as a story—a story that collects all of these moments, like the moment I shared with my students in Lake Superior, when our capacity to comprehend who we are and who God is becomes more expansive. The Bible is these moments compiled together in a way that reveals that in their collective total, they have a trajectory. They evolve. They move forward.

We know this is true about the Bible because it is also true about our lives.

THE BIG STORY

We can't assume that we all come from traditions that value "story" or intuitively see the narrative of Scripture, or that if we do, we see it the same way. If reading the Bible as story is new to you, don't get overwhelmed by the concept or overcomplicate it. All you need to do is keep in mind as you read the Bible that there is more unity than there is disunity to the Bible. And that overall, the sum total of the scriptures is moving forward in one direction. Some ways to describe this story progression in chapters, acts, or movements include:

- Creation, Fall, Redemption

- Creation, Fall, Redemption, New Creation

- Creation, Fall, Israel, Church, New Creation

- Creation, Fall, People, Tribe, Kingdom, Exile, Incarnation, Church, New Creation

These words simply act as metaphorical containers or placeholders for marking how and when the story of the Bible moves forward. Whatever framework works for you, your students, and your tradition, it may be helpful to create an image to put on the wall of your youth room or ask students to create an artistic representation of the story. Or work together with your students on how to tell the story of the Bible using the words and symbols that are most helpful to them. Whenever you're reading the Bible on your own or with your students, locate the story you're reading in the context of the larger story in the way that you see it and understand it. If you're looking for further resources on the "Big Story" of the Bible and how we read it, check out the following books.

- Craig Bartholomew and Michael Goheen, *The True Story of the Whole World: Finding Your Place in the Biblical Drama*

- Lisa Sharon Harper, *The Very Good Gospel: How Everything Wrong can be Made Right*

- Scot McKnight, *The Blue Parakeet: Rethinking How You Read the Bible*

- Michael Novelli, *Shaped by the Story: Helping Students Encounter God in a New Way*

- Anne Streaty Wimberly, *Soul Stories: African American Christian Education*

- N.T. Wright, *Scripture and the Authority of God: How to Read the Bible Today*

OUR STORIES

We make choices every day that have both small and large impact on the world around us. Most of us, if we're honest, live lives that lack critical thinking or space for helpful reflection. We live trapped in day-to-day rhythms and routines. We do good. We do evil. We do small tasks. We do large tasks. We speak kind words. We speak meaningless words. We spend money. We spend time. But we may have little idea why we are who we are or why we're becoming the kind of people we're becoming.

As the ancient philosopher Socrates famously warned, "The unexamined life is not worth living." Another way to say that might be: An intentional life doesn't happen by accident. There is no greater example of this reality than the life of the average adolescent. The high demands placed on our young people, along with the round-the-clock schedules imposed on them, make it nearly impossible for adolescents to live any other way than reactively.

When you ask a young person why they made a certain decision, they might respond, "I don't know." Adults can often interpret this as being dismissive or disrespectful, when in fact it could be one of the most honest statements our students can make.

When a young person makes a wise or foolish decision, adults often want to focus on that specific action. We make behavior "the thing" that matters most. But when we do this, we fail to recognize that there is always a "thing behind the thing." One path to beginning to examine our own lives, and to invite our students to do the same, is to acknowledge that behind every choice a person makes and every action a person takes are thoughts and feelings that inform those actions.

But behind all of those thoughts and feelings is another layer to who we are as people. These are the answers to basic questions about our own existence and the way we tell ourselves our own story. The way our story is told to us by our families and communities. The words we use, the actions we take, the people we share our lives with, and how we spend our time and money are manifestations of this deeper layer or level, the questions we're all asking and that propel all of our lives. We gain more access to the life God made us to live by becoming aware of how the basic root questions about our lives are shaping the kind of people we're becoming.

We gain more access to the life God made us to live by becoming aware of how the basic root questions about our lives are shaping the kind of people we're becoming.

Our society provides countess options for all of us, and specifically young people, to identify ourselves: through achievement, race, economic status, family name, gifts, talents, or with individuals or specific groups of people. This is because one of the questions common to the human experience that transcends age, time, and culture, is one of identity.

Namely, "Who am I?"[2]

Our answers to the question, "Who am I?" lead to specific thoughts, feelings, and actions. For example, when someone answers the question, "Who am I?" with a response communicating something like "unlovable," we shouldn't be surprised when he or she is plagued with negative thoughts, feels depressed, and ultimately makes repeated choices that reflect an "unlovable" identity.

The questions we're asking—and the ways we're finding answers—influence the people we're becoming.

However, the call of the Gospel is to live our story within God's great story, not just seeking to answer the question "Who am I?" at one point in time, but continually answering this question with another question: "Who is God?"

---

2 Three questions every human being is implicitly and explicitly asking and trying to answer through everything they think, feel, and do, are "Who am I?" [Identity], "What is my place?" [Belonging], and "Why am I here?" [Mission, or Purpose]. These three questions, in some form, have been foundational to how I practice ministry for over a decade. It's important to note that while we distinguish between the Identity, Belonging, and Purpose questions, they're often impossible for young people to pursue in isolation from one another. "Who am I?" is always connected with "What is my place?" "Who are the people around me?" "To what family, tribe, and people group do I belong?" "How do we make meaning together, and how do we make a way of life together?" For adolescents, that question is often tinged with rejection and a sense of being outside. They are driven by a desire to belong. More on these questions can be found in *Growing Young: 6 Essential Strategies to Help Young People Discover and Love Your Church* by Kara Powell, Jake Mulder, and Brad Griffin (Baker Books, 2016).

WHO AM I? WHO IS GOD?

Exodus 2 introduces the reader to the child of slaves who was meant to die in a massive genocide. Thanks to the work of several courageous women, he is rescued and then adopted into the Egyptian royal family, only later to commit murder and flee to a neighboring land. The Moses we find in Exodus 3 has been displaced from two families, two people groups, and his home country. He has committed a crime and is forced to live in exile, a refugee among strangers. These strangers welcome him and wrap him into a new family; he marries and has children.

In Exodus 3, when God meets Moses on Mount Sinai in the form of a burning bush and commissions him to lead the Israelites out of Egypt, it's no surprise that Moses' response is, "Who am I?" His life is a picture of an identity crisis. God's response is that God will go with him, leading to Moses' next question:

"Who is God?"

In order for Moses to choose to change the course of his life and to accept God's call to bring deliverance to the Israelites, he needs to revisit the question, "Who am I?" The first helpful response to this question is to ask about God's identity. The rest of the biblical story, including the "backstory" in the Book of Genesis, is the response to these two questions.

Who am I? Who is God?

I would argue that every story in the Bible was composed as a way of trying to offer a response to these two questions. We're invited to read the Bible as the evolving story of humanity attempting to ask and answer these two questions, reading the Bible as both theology and anthropology.

These two questions are the fuel that drive the redemptive story forward, ultimately climaxing in the life, death, resurrection, and ascension of Jesus Christ, who demonstrates the asking and answering of the questions, "Who am I?" and "Who is God?" Being fully human, Jesus is the ultimate demonstration of what it means to be human as God intended. And John 1 and Hebrews 1 show us that being fully God, Jesus is the clearest window through which we can understand the mystery of the divine. Jesus' identity confronts humanity with the asking and answering of these two questions.

"In the past, God spoke through the prophets to our ancestors in many times and many ways. In these final days, though, he spoke to us through a Son. God made his Son the heir of everything and created the world through him. The Son is the light of God's glory and the imprint of God's being."

HEBREWS 1:1-3

In the beginning was the Word
and the Word was with God
and the Word was God.
The Word was with God in the beginning.
The Word became flesh
and made his home among us.
We have seen his glory,
glory like that of a father's only son,
full of grace and truth.
No one has ever seen God.
God the only Son,
who is at the Father's side,
has made God known.

JOHN 1:1-2, 14, 18

When we grasp the power of these questions as the backdrop of the Bible as story, we're then able to unlock a method of interpreting the Bible that provides a more helpful reading of the Bible and of our own lives. In reading a narrative about King David, for example, the point of the story isn't that the reader merely ought to imitate King David. The point of the Torah or the commands in the Epistles isn't to dictate a formula for managing our individual sins and behaviors. While there are specific instructions in Scripture, along with histories, meditations, prayers, and prophecies, the ultimate direction of these collected writings is to provide answers to these two big questions within the context of the larger biblical narrative as it intersects with our lives, and therefore to transform our identities as followers of Jesus.

HOW WE READ THE BIBLE AS STORY

The "Who am I?" and "Who is God?" questions are the questions to ask when we encounter any story, poem, prophecy, or proverb in Scripture. In this approach, when we read these passages, we ask:

How does this story answer the question, "Who am I?"

- What do we find out about the nature of the characters in this story? How might that help us understand their—and our—answer to the question, "Who am I?" and the connected question, "Who are we?"

- How does this part of the story relate to other parts of the biblical story and the ways the "Who am I?" question is answered?

How does this story answer the question, "Who is God?"

- What do we find out about the nature of God in this story?

- How might that help us understand the characters'—and our—relationship to God?

- How does this part of the story relate to other parts of the biblical story and how God is revealed?

Reading the Bible using these questions will take some time and a lot of practice. I'm constantly re-centering myself on these questions because, at times, they are so contrary to the ways many of us learned to read the Bible or to the traditional interpretations of texts that we've received. Sometimes, the place to start may be the most obvious. When the story explicitly answers the "Who am I?" and "Who is God?" questions, be sure to take notes.

In response to the question, "Who am I?" you'll begin to see words like

image,

beloved,

rescued,

and child.

And in response to the question, "Who is God?" you might see words like

almighty,

potter,

mother hen,

and farmer.

While it's true that the Bible provides concrete answers to these two questions, we need to keep working to move beyond the obvious answers. If you're only ending up with lists, answers, and columns, you're likely missing out on the depth of the story. Asking and answering these questions may only lead to our asking and answering them again. This is a cyclical journey of asking and answering these questions again and again as we read and re-read the Bible.

Let's give it a try.

Many of us were taught that the point of the King David story is for us to "be like King David." But as one of our students once asked, "When are we supposed to be like King David? When he's defeating Goliath or when he's committing adultery?" This question reveals the limitations of the ways we may read biblical stories.

> *"When are we supposed to be like King David? When he's defeating Goliath or when he's committing adultery?"*

If we read the story of King David through the questions above, we see an evolving image of a God who is gracious and faithful to a man whose identity is a mixed bag of passion, giftedness, beauty, and brokenness. We see a story taking place early on in the unfolding of God's movement toward the restoration of all things.

So maybe the point of this story isn't that I ought to be like King David, but that the faithfulness and graciousness of God I see in his story can become a foundation for the ways I uniquely live out my own story. The answer to the question, "Who is God?" in King David's story can transform how I answer, "Who am I?" in my story.

And the process of asking and answering these questions as we read the Bible begins again.

INVITING OUR STUDENTS INTO THE STORY BY CREATING ENVIRONMENTS FOR GROWTH

As youth workers, we must embrace our role as ambassadors for the question, "Who am I?", modeling the reality that asking and answering this question is a lifelong process. The truth is that as soon as one of our students answers this question, she will likely find herself in a situation where she's forced to ask the question again. Asking questions can feel dangerous for students in religious settings where adults appear to be overly confident about what they believe. Therefore, your first task may be proactively working to create a safe, imaginative, and fearless environment. Then you can begin exploring the ways your programming and curriculum implicitly and explicitly engage the questions, "Who am I?" and "Who is God?"

Creating an appropriate growth environment may be your most crucial role as a youth worker. You can't manufacture this process and you can't do it for your students. As we've noted, they're already asking and answering these questions whether they realize it or not. And I think we can all agree that when our students experience growth and transformation, it is the work of the Spirit in their lives. All we can do as youth workers is provide age-appropriate and inclusive environments that are conducive to growth and discovery as students explore the questions they are (in some way) already asking.

When we think about *environments* for formation, I think it's important to think about them in at least two dimensions.

The first is the physical aspect of an environment.
While I wholeheartedly believe that all of life and all of creation is sacred, I also believe that one of the ways we come to experience and understand this is through the acknowledgement of some sort of sacred space. Especially with young people, sacred space disrupts the normal pattern and routine of their lives. It provides a wake-up call to greater awareness. For students, it's a reminder that they're even wearing sandals in the first place, and now might be a good time to take them off.

How does the physical space you invite your students into contrast with the space they experience throughout the rest of their day and week?

- Is it more or less noisy?

- Is it more or less creative?

- Is it more or less visually distracting?

- Is it more or less soothing?

- Does it feel safe, inviting, and open to all people?

- Are there explicit or implicit requirements for entry that would prevent anyone from entering with an open heart?

- Does it create space where students can encounter silence, stillness, and awe?

It's striking to me that the very environments into which we most often invite our young people make it nearly impossible for them to have the kinds of experiences we know they desperately need. With the best of intentions, many of the environments I created early in my work with young people included loud music, a full schedule, high stimulation, and no clear way for visitors to be integrated into the life of the community I was hoping to cultivate. I was inadvertently giving my students more of what many of them were experiencing in every other space of their lives.

In time, I learned that our youth group could offer an alternative environment to what many students were experiencing throughout their day and one that would be more inviting to experiencing the Bible as story. Lowering the volume in our student room and starting a hospitality team to help set up a welcoming space, meeting in the park down the street, going on a walk through a neighborhood that our students have never experienced, or getting away to a different location can be disruptive enough to provide the sort of environment that is conducive to exploring these questions.

The second is the relational aspect of an environment. More than the physical space of your youth room, the relationships adults have with students—and students have with one another—will be the soil out of which God grows and transforms lives. For clarity, a relational environment is more than just creating small group time in your program. It is the hidden curriculum that happens in between more overt aspects of programming and youth ministry structures. It is how you listen, respect, suspend judgment, and voice response in every interaction you have with your students.

- Are you and the other adults who are part of your youth ministry aware of the ways you're asking and answering big questions?

- Are you at least a few steps farther along on the spiritual journey than your students?

- Is there a depth and maturity to the kinds of relationships you're building with students that would create the space for students to process their lives and these questions with you?

- And, if students are willing to ask these questions with you, have you developed the wisdom to know when and when not to answer them?

When young people ask questions, we can feel pressure to provide quick and definitive answers. If our students are brave enough to wrestle openly with questions related to their identity, we instinctively want to tell them who they are or who they should be. However, rather than providing a quick response, we can have a lasting impact by allowing them to ask and answer this question through self-discovery, communal discernment, and the work of the Spirit in their lives as they read the Bible as story. We can affirm the asking and answering of this question as common to the human experience, and invite them to begin discovering answers by asking the question, "Who is God?" as the answer to both of these questions are revealed in the story of the Bible and the person of Jesus Christ. (We'll explore the value of question-asking further in chapter 6.)

When we have the courage to ask "Who am I?" and "Who is God?" with our students, we invite them to participate in a journey that is rooted in the Bible as story and has been unfolding throughout history.

This is a dynamic process of discovery—some refer to it as "transformation," "spiritual growth," or "spiritual formation"—that keeps on repeating, growing, and maturing. During this process, the journey with our students is as important as the destination. The asking of the questions is as important as the answers. And to participate in this process is to participate in what the Bible actually is, the sacred stories of humans asking and answering these questions throughout history.

Encouraging the asking and answering of these two questions propels our students on a lifelong faith process. This opportunity invites us as leaders to move past our focus on the immediate behaviors and actions of our students, and to engage them in the process of examining and re-examining their lives as they pursue the way of Jesus.

So we join students where they are and share life with them.

We help students ask the *next* question.

We guide them to find and trust God through every question, answer, and experience.

And we continually invite students to believe the Good News: The answers to the questions "Who am I?" and "Who is God?", which drive the entire story of the Bible, are found in the person of Jesus Christ.

TRY THIS ... IN YOUR LIFE:

- When have you experienced moments of awe and wonder like the one described at the beginning of this chapter? How did it impact your life?

- Buy a new journal and on the front page write the question, "Who am I?" and on the back page write, "Who is God?" Spend the next season logging responses to these two questions.

- How would you describe the "Bible as Story"? Take time to write or draw your understanding of the story from beginning to end.

- Ask some respected friends, colleagues, or mentors how they would describe their place in the story of the Bible, and how they came to that conclusion.

- Reflect on the people, places, or events that have shaped how you might answer the questions "Who am I?" and "Who is God?"

TRY THIS ... IN YOUR MINISTRY:

- Cover the walls of your youth group meeting space with blank paper. Ask students to write out or draw their understanding of the story of the Bible.

- Give your students and leaders poster boards or large pieces of cardstock paper. On one side invite them to come up with as many responses to the question, "Who am I?" as possible, and on the other side invite them to come up with as many responses to the question, "Who is God?" as possible. Keep these in a safe place, and on a semi-regular basis, get them out and let students add new responses and reflect on what they previously wrote.

- Work to create intentional moments of awe and wonder for your students and volunteers. Go outside, embark on adventures, sit in darkness, or visit a cemetery. Do whatever it takes.

- Review your existing curriculum and training materials, looking for anything that teaches the Bible as story. If you can't find it, consider modifying your approach to incorporate the two big questions.

- As a ministry team, consider that each one of a student's actions is connected to a thought or a feeling, which is influenced by how a student might be asking or answering the questions "Who am I?" and "Who is God?" Develop a greater awareness of how your students' actions connect to their desire to find their place in a bigger story.

WHEN SHOULD WE ASK THESE QUESTIONS?

In chapter 2 we discussed "Four Crucial Questions to Help Students Consider what the Bible is Asking of Them." These four questions have proven incredibly helpful when trying to read the Bible as commands, and when discerning how and which specific commandments might impact us as individuals and as a community. However, the Bible isn't only a list of commands, it is also a story, and how we read the Bible as story demands a different set of questions. More practically, if you're trying to discern an appropriate response to a specific commandment or rule, the questions from chapter 2 will help you read the Bible in this way. If you're trying to make sense of a story in Scripture in the larger story of the Bible and your place in it, the questions in this chapter will help you read in this way.

So, when should we ask "Who am I?" and "Who is God?"

On one level, most of us are already asking and answering these questions whether we realize it or not. And just like all of us are asking and answering the question, "Who am I?" with everything we're doing, thinking, and feeling every day, the writers of the Bible are attempting to ask and answer "Who am I?" and "Who is God?" with much of the story of Scripture.

I've found that many of us have been trained to try to "boil down" every story in the Bible to a point or an application. We want to be able to clearly answer, "What does this mean for me or my students today?" This is an understandable impulse as we try to help our students engage Scripture and impact their lives (not to mention lead a small group). However, we need to recognize that we're imposing this question—and often many others—on the Bible. By taking that approach, we run the risk of missing out on what the Bible might be saying, and may be doing violence to the text.

But when we become aware that these two questions are already underneath, or embedded in, each story, and we allow them to shine through the text, we often will see the story expand. As these questions expand a story, rather than boil it down, they can lead to various possibilities for each of our lives, rather than one prescribed application, as we wrestle with the same questions in our own different stories. For example, rather than saying, "the point of this story is to be like King David," sorting through what the specific story might reveal about how David was answering the questions, "Who am I?" and "Who is God?" can have all sorts of implications for how we answer these questions in our own lives and with our students.

While this method can feel messier than a more formulaic or systematic approach to applying the Bible to our lives, it can prevent us from missing the story for the sake of an application, while also giving us much more imaginative possibilities for helping our students find their place in the "Big Story" of the Bible.

6

QUESTIONS TO ASK

"And what about you? Who do you say that I am?"

MATTHEW 16:15

SO MANY QUESTIONS

"What is the Bible?"

"How should we read it?"

These were some of the questions posed by our class of evangelical Christians taking the "Jewish Thought and Practice" course in Israel that I mentioned in chapter 4.

Early on in the class, we were exploring Jewish perspective on the Bible and its interpretation, and an older woman kept asking the rabbi about inerrancy, a word with which he was not familiar. The rabbi graciously entertained our questions, but it was clear that his relationship with the Bible was far different from ours.

One of our homework assignments was to read the story of the "Akedah," the binding of Isaac in Genesis 22. We were asked to list as many questions as we could about this story. I thought this assignment was interesting, because any other assignment I'd ever received about the Bible had always involved reading a passage and then spending all my energy composing a paper explaining what I thought it meant to the original audience and what it means now. We were supposed to explain a passage, take a position, and defend it.

This assignment was different. The rabbi asked us to read a passage and then let it speak for itself, and to write down as many questions as came to mind.

As I read the story of the binding of Isaac, I realized how difficult this assignment was for someone trained to read the Bible the way I had been. While I absorbed the details of the story, my mind automatically tried to summarize it, gloss over the awkward parts, and connect the story to Jesus. But when we immediately interpret this narrative as a foreshadowing of Jesus' death and resurrection, it's difficult to read the authentic story.

We do this all the time. We read and teach about stories with a preconceived notion of what the Bible is, how we're supposed to read it, how it fits together, and what it's supposed to mean. We miss out on the complexity of the real stories, and the stories aren't able to speak for themselves.

Absorbing a story and asking questions was harder than I anticipated.

So, I worked hard to stick with the general, Who? What? When? Where? Why? and How? sorts of questions.

I came up with a list of ten or eleven questions, and even though I had answers to most of them, I felt confident about my list. Surely, I had the most extensive list of questions compared to all of my classmates.

When we arrived at class a few days later, the rabbi asked us all to share our questions. We each read through our list. Many of our questions were similar, and we all brought under a dozen questions. The rabbi listened to each of us attentively, never interjecting or writing anything down.

After the last student shared, the rabbi stood up and said,

"That's it? Those are all the questions you have? You are so lucky! I have *so many questions*!"

Then he opened up his Bible and read the story to our class, and he began to list all of his questions. His questions weren't about, "When did this happen?" and "Where was Abraham when God told him to do this?" But instead were about, "What kind of God would ask a man to kill his own son?" and, "What kind of person would just listen?"

His questions were more accusatory in nature. They cut to the heart of our assumptions about who God is and what it means to be human. These were not questions that would have been asked in the classroom of my Bible school or any of our churches back home, because we already knew the answers. The only answer to, "What kind of God?" was, "A loving God." Which, at face value, doesn't make that much sense in this particular story.

Those sorts of canned answers seemed like rubbish in the face of the rabbi's intensity, and the mystery of the story we had encountered.

The rabbi was only interested in the questions.

Absolutely zero time or effort was spent on trying to answer any of the questions raised that day. This could have been, in part, because our questions weren't very good. But it was also because when we tried to answer his questions, he would interject and push us on to the next question.

His motive in this lesson was to teach us that questions have value in themselves. We were coming from religious traditions and perspectives where the point of the journey is the destination, and the point of the question is the answer. He was liberating us to find meaning in not just the answers but also the journey and the questions.

Reading the Bible with this rabbi was like reading the Bible again for the first time. Suddenly it contained nuance and depth, beauty and complexity. We were allowing it to be what it was and we were entering into a relationship with the text. We were respecting it enough to believe that it could be questioned, and that none of our questions were threats to the Bible or to God.

> *We were respecting the Bible enough to believe that it could be questioned, and that none of our questions were threats to the Bible or to God.*

Reading the Bible as a book of *questions to be asked* dramatically shifted my spiritual journey.

It invited me to ask, pushed me past the provided answers, provoked a spirit of curiosity, and helped me see beyond a dualistic "either/or" perspective. The Bible became endlessly and beautifully more complex. It was no longer a riddle to be solved or a puzzle to be put together. It became more of a mystery, because there are always more questions to be asked and there is always something else toward which a story could be pointing.

QUESTIONS AND ANSWERS

My experience with young people has taught me that they're filled with more questions than we could possibly imagine. Young people often find themselves feeling like the rabbi when they hear us talk about God and the Bible, and might even want to scream back at us, "That's it? Those are all the questions you have? You are so lucky! I have *so many questions!*"

According to research conducted by the Fuller Youth Institute, about seven of every ten high school students admit to struggling with doubts, but only one or two of those ten are likely to have had helpful conversations about those doubts with youth leaders or friends during high school.[1] This means that for one reason or another, we're not cultivating the types of environments and relationships that are conducive to young people expressing their questions and doubts.

It also means there's likely a lot of unexpressed doubt floating around in our youth ministries.

I wonder how many of the answers we provide to young people are to questions they aren't even asking. And I wonder how often our best attempts to give permission to our students to ask questions result in our providing

---

1 Kara Powell, Brad M. Griffin, and Cheryl Crawford, *Sticky Faith Youth Worker Edition: Practical Ideas to Nurture Long-Term Faith in Teenagers*, 144.

quick, clean, and safe answers. It's like we're saying, "Yes, you can ask that, as long as you accept the answers we provide." Which might be why they're not bringing their real questions to our youth groups.

Asking questions is a spiritual practice that youth workers need to reclaim. It needs to be both modeled and taught to our young people. After studying in Israel, I realized that I didn't have to travel across the world to learn this way of reading the Bible—it was actually already evident inside the Bible itself, in the life and teachings of Jesus.

JESUS IS THE ~~ANSWER~~ QUESTION

The method my rabbi-professor modeled and taught didn't just unlock something about the Bible, it unlocked for me a new experience of who Jesus was and is. As I began re-reading the teachings of Jesus, I started imagining him as someone like my instructor: kind, patient, passionate, slightly irreverent, and filled with questions. The rabbi always had an agenda for what he wanted to teach our class. He was highly prepared. But he had mastered the art of asking questions that provoked us to ask questions, and responded to our questions with more questions that exposed our motives, desires, and agendas.

Once you have eyes to see this, the Gospels reveal Jesus as a Jewish rabbi who also had mastered this method. Throughout the Gospels, Jesus asks and responds to hundreds of questions.

In one of the largest portions of Jesus' recorded teachings we have available, what is known as the Sermon on the Mount (Matthew 5-7), Jesus peppers his discourse with questions:

"But if the salt loses its saltiness, how can it be made salty again?"

And

"If you love those who love you, what reward will you get?"

And

"If you greet only your own people, what are you doing more than others?"

And

"Can any one of you by worrying add a single hour to your life?"

And

"Why do you worry about clothes?"

And

"Why do you look at the speck of sawdust in your brother's eye and pay no attention to the plank in your own eye?"

And

"Do people pick grains from thorn bushes, or figs from thistles?"

Jesus doesn't just ask questions as a rhetorical device to make his point. He also interacts with the questions of those around him as an invitation to go further. Some of Jesus' most memorable teachings began with someone else's questions.

We wouldn't have the well-known parable of the Good Samaritan in Luke 10 if the expert in the law hadn't asked Jesus,

"Who is my neighbor?"

We wouldn't have the dramatic teaching about wealth and the Kingdom of God in Luke 18 if the rich young ruler hadn't asked Jesus,

"What must I do to inherit eternal life?"

And we wouldn't have Jesus' bold reframing of sin and suffering in John 9 if the disciples hadn't asked,

"Who sinned, this man or his parents?"

But Jesus doesn't only use people's questions as a springboard for his teachings. He also is interested in their motives. He responds to their questions by asking more questions, to cut to the heart of those he's trying to teach.

For example, in Matthew 17, Jesus responds to Peter's loaded question with another loaded question (vv. 24-25):

> When they came to Capernaum, the people who collected the half-shekel temple tax came to Peter and said, "Doesn't your teacher pay the temple tax?"

"Yes," he said.

But when they came into the house, Jesus spoke to Peter first. "What do you think, Simon? From whom do earthly kings collect taxes, from their children or from strangers?"

In Mark 10 Jesus responds to the Pharisees' question about marriage by essentially asking them if they've ever read the scriptures (vv. 2-3):

Some Pharisees came and, trying to test him, they asked, "Does the Law allow a man to divorce his wife?"

Jesus answered, "What did Moses command you?"

In Luke 6 Jesus challenges traditional interpretations of the time period in his response to the Pharisees' question about his Sabbath practices (vv.2-3):

Some Pharisees said, "Why are you breaking the Sabbath law?"

Jesus replied, "Haven't you read what David and his companions did when they were hungry?

And in some of the most intense moments of Jesus' life, rather than overtly proclaiming what is true, he invites those around him to discover it on their own.

During a climactic exchange with Peter in Caesarea Philippi in Matthew 16, Jesus asks:

"Who do people say the Son of Man is?" and "What about

you? Who do you say that I am?" (vv. 13, 15, NIV)

And in John 18 when Jesus is on trial, Pilate asks him:

"Are you the King of the Jews?"

Jesus responds by saying,

"Do you say this on your own or have others spoken to you about me?" (vv. 33-34)

Through his life and teaching, Jesus models a method of asking questions that reveals a desire for those around him to take their next step on the journey of discovery and growth. What could that next step look like for us and for our students?

A SPIRITUALITY OF ASKING QUESTIONS

Most of the experiences our young people have had in schools and in church have taught them that inquiry leads to an answer, and that there is always a right answer. It's likely not difficult for most of us to remember sitting in school, wishing our teachers would just tell us the answer so we could get it right on a test and move on.

This approach isn't all bad, but it has limited effectiveness in stimulating spiritual insights. Answers often end the conversation. Questions often lead to growth. The art of asking questions and allowing questions to remain unresolved will be counterintuitive to many of us as

Answers often end the conversation. Questions often lead to growth.

leaders and to most of our students.

When I first started serving as a high school pastor, the church I was serving held small groups during the school year, and then offered six weeks of alternative programming in the summer. In the past, this six weeks of programming had been more "event" or "attractional" in nature, which served the ministry and students well. The summer programming didn't involve small groups in order to give our leaders a break from the grind of weekly programming. Student participation and attendance was also sporadic every summer.

However, I had a sense that summer could be a good opportunity to go even further with the "question asking" that we hoped to teach and model to our students. So, we announced that our summer programming would simply be, "Summer Bible Study," which wasn't totally accurate. While we wanted our students to learn about the Bible, we were more interested in their learning how to ask questions. Before you judge the lack of creative marketing behind the name "Summer Bible Study," compare it to "Summer Question Asking" and decide which you like better (or which would be more convincing to students' parents).

During the first week, we showed all our cards. We gave them an outline of the format for each of our gatherings for the rest of the summer. We generally followed this rhythm:

- Students gathered in groups of three or four

and read the passage out loud as a group. This particular summer we looked at a different parable each week. Parables serve as great texts for asking a lot of questions.

- As a group, students wrote down as many questions as possible. We assured them that there is no such thing as a bad question or an obvious question.

- Each group then shared their list of questions with the larger group, while a couple of other students and I recorded all of the questions on a giant whiteboard.

- If the same question was asked multiple times, we underlined it every time.

- We worked hard to demonstrate our enthusiasm for the questions being asked. We reminded everyone that judgment or snickering about questions wouldn't be tolerated.

- Once all of the questions were collected on the whiteboard, we asked students to identify connections and correlations, to see if there were any common themes that revealed what the most people were the most curious about.

- After several themes were identified, we decided as a group which questions we wanted to discuss. It was frustrating to everyone that we revealed and validated hundreds of questions but only ended up exploring a few of them. However, it was also a clear example of the Bible's richness and depth.

- We then spent the rest of our time discussing the one theme we had decided on. I did my best to connect ideas and offer some practical invitations based on the text and the theme, but I also did my best to respond to the question, and the subsequent questions of the students, with more questions.

It took us a few weeks to get into this rhythm, but for several years we followed the same pattern in the summer. Students and adults alike fell in love with this method. As I look back on my time as a youth pastor with that community, I point to this initiative as one of the most meaningful experiences I had with students. I had to be vulnerable about my own questions. I had to be quick on my feet for 120 minutes, not knowing where the experience or conversation would lead. I had to be prepared, having studied as much as I could about the story I was inviting students to read. If I was going to host their questions well, I had to have a knowledge diverse enough that I would not unintentionally steer the conversation toward my own preconceived ideas.

This experiment demanded a lot of me as a leader, and stepping into this method of asking questions challenged me in several ways.

1. QUESTIONS REQUIRE VULNERABILITY.

So many of us are afraid of our own questions or our students' questions because they make everything about our lives and our faith less certain than what we like to project. Our questions reveal as much about us as they reveal about the Bible. They reveal our motives and our agenda, the shortcomings of our worldviews, our deepest fears and desires, our theological perspectives, our opinions, our imagination, and our lack of imagination.

Our questions or the questions of our young people force us to reveal our intent in a way that we're not normally comfortable with, but it is exactly this kind of vulnerability that invites all of us into environments often most conducive to transformation. Appropriate vulnerability looks different in every context, and you could get yourself in trouble in this area if you don't know the culture of your community or don't have the support of your team. I'd highly recommend running the questions and doubts you're considering sharing by your team, and possibly your supervisor, so they can help you think of the potential risks involved and help sharpen and nuance what it is you'd like to share. The risk of vulnerability is worth taking, but we should be as strategic as possible.

2. QUESTIONS CREATE SPACE.

If you're reading this and thinking, "Wow, I have a lot of questions, and I hope my senior pastor doesn't find out," then you may be acknowledging that there is not adequate or healthy space in your job and community for you to explore and grow in your relationship with God and the Bible.

If this is how you feel, just imagine how your students feel.

I'm not saying that this is a good reason for you to quit serving as a youth leader tomorrow, but it may cause you to pause and reflect on the ways your students may and *may not* be experiencing God and the Bible. Shifting this culture in your ministry and your church likely starts with you taking the risk of modeling what it looks like to have and ask questions. It could put you in a tricky position, but it could also create the exact kind of experience your students may need. The questions Jesus asked always created space for those he encountered to grow.

CAN I ASK THAT?

If we are going to answer that question with a "Yes" that is both pastorally compassionate and responsible, we have to know our environment and context. Some theological and cultural traditions are more hesitant—and even resistant—to engaging with "tough" questions. In some environments, inviting young people to ask questions can be interpreted as disrespecting authority. While on the one hand this hesitancy reflects a deep and beautiful appreciation for authority, on the other hand, it may also reveal a personal or theological insecurity that may exist in a particular leader or religious community. As you consider inviting your students into the practice of asking questions, consider the following:

1. Test your ideas on how to invite students to ask questions with your senior pastor, colleagues, volunteers, and parents. This is even more important if you've recently joined your community or you're a theological or cultural outsider. The wisdom and feedback you gain from them will go a long way toward improving the experience you offer students, understanding the concerns of adults, garnering buy-in from key people, and protecting you from any pushback that comes your way from initiating this practice. Even if you decide to proceed with some of your new ideas, at the very least you will have a better sense of potential obstacles ahead.

2. Tell stories of transformation from your own life and the lives of others in your community that include asking questions and exploring doubts. Even in contexts that are resistant to asking questions, you likely will be able to find someone who is willing to lend their story for the sake of the young people in your community.

3. If the resistance is too great, this invitation to your students may have to come more "from the side" (during one-on-one conversations, coffee shop meetings, and

discussion before or after programming) than "from the front" as a regular part of your ministry programming.

For more on this topic, check out the *Can I Ask That?* curriculum resources from the Fuller Youth Institute.

3. QUESTIONS REQUIRE NEW SKILLS.

If this way of learning about God and the Bible runs against the grain of how many of our students have been taught, then that is likely true for you as well. It was for me.

My default setting was to respond quickly to every question my students asked with an answer. I thought that's what they wanted, and I'll be honest, it always feels good during those rare occasions when you're able to put your Bible school classes, seminary education, or your own Bible study to use.

For me, there came a time when I decided that before I responded to any question from a student, leader, or parent, I would take two deep breaths. Sometimes this felt a little awkward for everyone involved, but it dramatically shifted how I *responded* to people when they asked me a question.

I use the word "respond" very intentionally, because this

practice shifted my behavior from "answering" students' questions to "responding" to students' questions. Sometimes I responded with an answer, but I was also learning to respond with more questions. Surprisingly, this practice also increased the frequency with which my response to people's questions was, "I don't know." The brief pause between the questions and my responses allowed me the time to choose humility and nuance over pride and certainty. I still have so much room to grow in this skill, and I suspect I'm not alone in that.

Our students still talk about the freedom they experienced through all the questions we asked during Summer Bible Study. And the insights from the questions our students asked several years ago still inform my own study and teaching. One of the most effective sermons I've ever preached in my congregation started with saying, "All of the insight I'm sharing with you this morning I learned from the high school students in our church. The questions of our young people have so much to teach us."

It was—and still is—true.

TRY THIS ... IN YOUR LIFE:

- Try to remember the questions you had about God and the Bible when you were a child. Make a list, and try to remember how adults in your life answered these questions.

- Make a list of questions you feel like you're not allowed to ask, or would be too risky to ask publicly, in your current church or ministry setting.

- For a season, limit your devotional or Bible study practice to reading and listing as many questions as possible. Reflect on your questions and what they might reveal about yourself, about God, and about the Bible. Try not to answer them.

- Ask your pastor or a mentor about a time in their life when asking new questions transformed their spiritual journey.

- Try to go a designated amount of time without "answering" anybody's questions (maybe one hour, one day, or one week), but only responding with your own questions.

TRY THIS ... IN YOUR MINISTRY:

- Ask students to anonymously submit questions about God or the Bible that they're afraid to ask, and later share the list of questions with your youth group (be sure to let them know up front that you're going to share these questions, but not their names).

- At the end of every teaching or lesson, ask students to write down a question to share with the group or bring to their small group.

- Every time you teach your students about the Bible, include a list of questions you have about the passage (without answering all of them).

- Do a study or series on the Gospels that involves looking at every question that Jesus asks, and how he responds to all the questions people ask him.

- Examine your pool of usual "go-to" resources for Bible study and preparation. Try to diversify your options by including voices that inspire more curiosity or question asking (consider looking at the listed resources about the Old Testament or Jesus in the back of this book written by Jewish authors).

7

A WRESTLING MATCH

CAN WE STRUGGLE WITH GOD?

How long will you forget me, LORD? Forever?
How long will you hide your face from me?
How long will I be left to my own wits,
agony filling my heart? Daily?
How long will my enemy keep defeating me?
Look at me!
Answer me, LORD my God!
Restore sight to my eyes!

PSALM 13:1-3A

CARLY'S CALL

A couple of hours into a good conversation over coffee with a friend from out of town, I received a phone call from a number I didn't recognize.

It was Carly, one of my former students, calling from the hospital to tell me that her dad was being moved home to receive hospice care. She was pretty sure he only had a few days, if not mere hours, left to live.

Carly's dad had been a volunteer in our high school ministry for nearly a decade. Eighteen months earlier, he had been diagnosed with an aggressive and incurable form of brain cancer. After his diagnosis, Tom experienced a remarkable quality of life for a while. He watched Tom Petty perform live, walked his oldest daughter down the aisle at her wedding, and, astoundingly, kept volunteering in our high school ministry.

Tom was one of those volunteers you just can't imagine your ministry without. He was willing to do anything to help. He was optimistic and compassionate, and unwavering in his support of our pastors and the ministry we were developing. Tom loved working with young people, and I think he loved caring for people who loved working with young people even more. He was a volunteer whose role became to care for other volunteers, and he was exceptional at it. His volunteers loved him. After his diagnosis, and even during intense treatment, Tom kept showing up on Sunday nights for the students and leaders he loved so much. He was well known for telling people how "cool" he thought they were. Actually, Tom had a knack for talking about how "cool" everything was. His positivity and enthusiasm were contagious.

Just a month prior to receiving this phone call from Carly, we learned that the cancer had returned and was rapidly progressing. Tom courageously faced and survived a risky surgery, but he wasn't quite the same after, and we all had a sense that we were closer to the end of his story than we were ready to be.

Still, I wasn't prepared for the call. I told my friend I had to leave, and headed to Tom's house.

The time we shared was sacred. I don't know if Tom recognized me or knew who I was, but I was able to pray with him and his family, and to tell Tom how "cool" I thought he was. Saying goodbye to someone whose "hello" meant so much to so many in our community was beyond surreal.

A few days later, as my wife and I prepared for a summer gathering with our family, I received a text from Carly letting me know that Tom had passed away peacefully. She requested that I come meet with the family the following day. Even though Tom had told me several months earlier that he wanted me to officiate his funeral when the time came, my heart was finally catching up to my head, and I felt an overwhelming sense of dread.

How could I share words of comfort when I was feeling so much grief and pain?

What would I say to our students and volunteers?

How could I offer strength when I was feeling so much loss?

And how would I deal with all of the well-meaning comments that would be offered in an attempt to comfort those who were grieving? If anyone quoted Paul's words, "to live is Christ and to die is gain" (Philippians 1:21, NIV), I knew that I would scream!

Because nothing was gained at this moment by this wife without a husband, two daughters without a father, and a community without its greatest advocate for young people. *Nothing was gained by this loss.* Telling myself that I was "doing this for Tom" was the only thing that moved me toward preparing for the next few days.

I knew that part of my job would be to offer wisdom and guidance from the Bible during the funeral service. But I kept procrastinating that part of my preparation.

Sitting with Tom's family and friends felt real and important.

Reading my Bible was the last thing I wanted to do.

Thinking about verses declaring the promises of God, the goodness of God, and our future hope as Christians only made me angry.

Thinking about verses declaring the promises of God, the goodness of God, and our future hope as Christians only made me angry. I had absolutely zero energy for scouring the Bible for these kinds of verses. More than ever, verses about God, life, and faith weren't lining up with my real circumstances and emotions.

Have you been to a funeral, or in some other difficult or painful circumstance, where the pain and sorrow being experienced in the room was addressed by Bible verses intended to make you feel better? Maybe they talked about a faraway land, or that "somehow, it's better this way," and you wondered whether the person talking actually knew what just happened or what any of you were going through. Maybe you found yourself thinking,

"I can't swallow that pill."

Or

"I can't buy what they're selling."

Or

"I can't accept this as real."

Out of advocacy for your own emotions and those in the room who were feeling the same way, you wanted to scream, "Are you kidding? The only appropriate thing to say right now is that life sucks and this sucks!"

Why do we feel this way at moments like this?

Life's painful and brutal circumstances have a way of disrupting our best efforts to articulate a neat and tidy way of understanding reality, faith, and the Bible. This is one of the gifts that comes through suffering. In fact, suffering is a catalyst latent with the potential to change us and how we see and experience the world. I have come to believe that trauma has a unique way of disrupting our theology. It brings a precision and clarity to life that cuts to the heart of who we are and what we truly believe.

This is where things can get messy with the Bible.

In my experience, when we're facing suffering and tragedy, often we are presented with only two opposing options about faith and the Bible:

The first is to "believe the Bible."

Just trust the promises.

Believe in the goodness.

Know that this is all for the better.

And for some of us, during certain times and situations, this has been helpful.

But for many of us, this option feels like we're being forced to choose between honesty and faith. We're being forced to choose between our emotions, what we know to be true on an experiential level, and the beliefs we've been taught or are being told.

The second option is to *despair*.

Just walk away.

Believe there's no hope.

Know nothing but suffering and death.

You know, like those people "who don't have any hope." (1 Thessalonians 4:13)

Christians don't usually speak too highly of this second option for a number of reasons. On the surface, it seems much more harmful than the first. It's better if everyone just believes and trusts. But while the second option seems slightly more honest, we also can't settle into that space for long. It's just too dark, and we want to believe that our faith can offer us more than despair, while not having to accept dishonest niceties.

Is there another option?

A SMACKDOWN OF BIBLICAL PROPORTIONS

Early on in the Bible we meet Jacob, a complicated man with a complicated story. His name means "deceiver," and it fits his actions well. He steals the birthright of his older brother, Esau, and spends much of his adult life on the run.

After many years, Jacob finds himself ready to meet his brother once again. The evening before he meets Esau, the Bible paints this scene for us in Genesis 32:24-32 (NIV):

> So Jacob was left alone, and a man wrestled with him till daybreak. When the man saw that he could not overpower him, he touched the socket of Jacob's hip so that his hip was wrenched as he wrestled with the man. Then the man said, "Let me go, for it is daybreak."

But Jacob replied, "I will not let you go unless you bless me."

CHAPTER 7: A WRESTLING MATCH

The man asked him, "What is your name?"

"Jacob," he answered.

Then the man said, "Your name will no longer be Jacob, but Israel, because you have struggled with God and with humans and have overcome."

Jacob said, "Please tell me your name."

But he replied, "Why do you ask my name?" Then he blessed him there.

So Jacob called the place *Peniel*, saying, "It is because I saw God face to face, and yet my life was spared."

The sun rose above him as he passed *Peniel*, and he was limping because of his hip.

There are numerous ways of reading this passage, because it is one of those passages that can provoke so many good questions. Who is this "man" that Jacob wrestles with? Where did he come from? Was this common practice? And—hopefully—countless other questions.

Some say that Jacob was wrestling with a divine being— some kind of angel. Others say that Jacob was wrestling with God. Still others say that Jacob was wrestling with himself. Regardless of how you answer this question, some of the implications remain the same.

Many of Jacob's choices caused harm to himself and to countless others, and while his misfortune and the sins of others had led to his own suffering, these were the exact things that led him to this moment of wrestling. Jacob's real-life experience, all the good and all the bad, built up to this divine encounter.

God engages with Jacob in this struggle as an active participant. The name of God's chosen people, Israel, means "to wrestle" or "to struggle," implying that they are a people wrestling or struggling with God. Although Jacob walked away limping, he received a new name, which God gave to him as a blessing. In the midst of this suffering and wrestling, Jacob saw the face of God.

There is no Israel without Jacob.

There often is no growth without wrestling.

To be a person of God is often to be someone who wrestles with God.

There usually is no transformation without struggle.

Through this story, Jacob becomes an archetype for what the spiritual life looks like. To be a person of God is often to be someone who wrestles with God. We see this truth manifest itself in multiple stories throughout the Bible.

In Genesis 18:16-32, Abraham pleads with God to have mercy on the people of Sodom. God actually relents by lowering the requirement of fifty righteous people to ten righteous people in order to save the city. Ultimately, Abraham's bargaining and wrestling with God saved the lives of some of Lot's family.

In Exodus 32:9-14, the Israelites create a golden calf and participate in idol worship while Moses is still hanging out with God on Mt. Sinai. God becomes angry and contemplates destroying the Israelites, but Moses argues and pleads with God to remember Abraham, Isaac, and Jacob. While the Israelites weren't spared the wrath of Moses upon his return, Moses' audacity in his verbal argument with God protected the Israelites from God's wrath.

In 2 Kings 20:1-11, King Hezekiah became ill and was told by Isaiah the prophet that he would die in just a short time. Hezekiah's passionate tears and prayers caused God to add fifteen years to his life.

There is a book in the Hebrew Bible, or our Old Testament, called *Lamentations*. It is an entire book of complaints, accusations, and pleas from Jeremiah on behalf of the Israelites to God during their time of exile.

Out of 150 psalms in the Bible, at least 65 have been categorized as laments—cries demanding to be heard, asking God to act.

In Mark 14:32-42, while praying in solitude in the Garden of Gethsemane, Jesus pleads with God to "take this cup of suffering away from me." Luke's Gospel says Jesus prayed so desperately that his "sweat became like drops of blood falling on the ground" (Luke 22:44).

In the midst of his suffering on the cross in Matthew 27:46, Jesus cries out, "My God, my God, why have you forsaken me?" (NIV). His questioning of God is a dramatic example of Jesus' embodiment of this way of reading the Bible. Jesus is quoting from Psalm 22:1-2, a lament which in context reads:

> "My God, my God, why have you forsaken me?
> Why are you so far from saving me,
> so far from my cries of anguish?
> My God, I cry out by day, but you do not answer,
> by night, but I find no rest." (NIV)

In one of the most painful and excruciating circumstances a human being could ever experience, the divine Son of God, the Messiah of Israel, the rightful king of heaven and earth, quotes the Bible as a direct question and accusation against God. Jesus invites us into a radical interaction with the biblical text that doesn't deny our experience, but instead validates it as the fuel to wrestle with and rage against God in some of our darkest and most painful moments.

Jesus invites us into a radical interaction with the biblical text that doesn't deny our experience, but instead validates it as the fuel to wrestle with and rage against God in some of our darkest and most painful moments.

The Bible demands we wrestle with it. One of the most inspiring and unique aspects of the Bible is that it contains within its pages the affirmation of this struggle. Some of the most dynamic stories about God involve God's people struggling with God. Therapist and theologian Dan Allender writes, "It is inconceivable to surrender to God, unless there is a prior, declared war against him."[1]

All of this leads me to believe that we have more than two choices when it comes to reading the Bible in light of our pain. We don't have to swallow it—or simplistic interpretations of it—without struggle. And we don't have to walk away because we believe our struggle is symptomatic of some sort of lack of faith or that our pain is too deep for God, the Bible, and the church to handle.

LET THE GAMES BEGIN

When I let myself wonder about who might be most desperate to wrestle and struggle, I think of our students. My experience with teenagers has exposed me to more pain, suffering, trauma, questions, and doubt than I ever could have imagined. Our young people are holding together the tension and dynamism of their historically unprecedented complex lives, and are looking for an environment where they can be honest about it all and make sense of it all. Our young people are looking for permission to allow their lived experience to lead them into

---

1 Dan Allender, "The Hidden Hope in Lament", June 2, 2016. https://theallendercenter.org/2016/06/hidden-hope-lament/

a struggle with God. Our young people need us to validate their experience, not tell them to distrust it.

I've heard many well-meaning pastors and professors declare,

"We can't trust our experience, we can only trust the Bible."

And

"How you feel doesn't matter, because you have the promises of God."

This false dichotomy communicates to our students the exact opposite of the Bible's message and invitation. When we impose the Bible on our experience, we repress our emotions and we stifle our growth. We become stuck, and for many, this feeling of "stuck-ness" can cause us to despair or walk away from faith and the Bible altogether. Or, worse yet, it can leave us in a perpetual state of denial and immature faith. It's possible that people walk away from God and the Bible because we haven't helped them understand that it's big enough to embrace their actual experience and their stories of pain and suffering.

The Bible invites us to start with our experience and to move from there. To start with what we know in this moment to be true from our lives, and to engage the stories, wrestle with the ideas, and wrestle with God. We're invited to take the sum total of our sins and stories and selves and to fiercely engage with the text with as much honesty and energy as possible. When we engage with the Bible this way, we're participating in one aspect of what the Bible is—a record of the wrestling match that has been taking place between God and humanity since the beginning of time. When we read the Bible as a wrestling match, we participate in this ongoing struggle that transcends space and time, and is an essential part of what it means to be a growing and maturing person of faith.

So, what does this look like for you and your students?

Like most other suggestions in this book, the first place to start is with ourselves. I am a firm believer that we usually can't take people where we haven't gone, which means we have to wrestle with God and the Bible, or have wrestled with God and the Bible, if we want our students to have this experience. It's entirely possible that our students need us to take them to a place where we haven't yet had the opportunity, or courage, to go.

Your next steps can be difficult to prescribe, but they likely have less to do with the Bible and more to do with you. You may need to do some intense reflection and interior work on your own story before you can return to the Bible with a readiness to engage in this way. You could start by reflecting on the following questions:

- What have been some of the most difficult and painful experiences of my life?

- How did I deal with these experiences?

- What messages did I hear from other Christians about these experiences and how to deal with them?

- What role did the Bible play in how I dealt with these experiences?

- Did the way I engaged the Bible invite me into the depth of these experiences, or did it offer avoidance of these experiences?

- Have I ever endured trauma or suffering that I haven't talked about with another person or received professional support for (counseling, therapy, or support groups)?

- Have I ever expressed the true nature of my feelings about these experiences to God?

- If God were a human, how would I communicate with God about what I experienced and how I feel about it?

- Who in my life can I share these questions with, so I'm not asking them alone?

Creating some time and space to engage with and reflect on these questions may reveal to you if there are experiences in your life you have yet to fully process, and that may be the fuel for you to enter into a healthy, legitimate, and biblical struggle with God. Dropping our real-life challenges on the doorstep of the Bible with audacity and authenticity is not the opposite of faith, but an essential part of faith and participation in the Bible.

Here's what I mean:

The strength of the Bible may not be found only in its divine nature, but also in its human nature. It may not be found in its simplicity, but in its complexity. It may not be found in its sterility, but in its messiness. This is not to say that it isn't

"God-breathed," but the way in which it is "God-breathed" may challenge many of our default views on what that might mean.

God inspires words that include questioning of God. God exercises divine authority through stories that include arguments with and about God. God doesn't appear to have a fragile ego or struggle with insecurity. The nature of the Bible itself invites us to share our full human experience with God: all the joy, pain, suffering, victory, certainty, and doubt. All of these emotions are included in our sacred text, and all of these emotions we experience are sacred before God.

So maybe the question for many of us isn't, "Have I gone too far?" in my emotions, prayers, and audacity before God.

Maybe the question is, "Have I gone far enough?" and "Am I really being honest with myself and with God?"

Remember, on the other side of these divine wrestling matches is growth, blessing, and often, limping. Your newly acquired blessing, name, and limp will become a gift to your students and your ministry, a gift your students wouldn't be able receive without you having the courage and audacity to wrestle with God all night. Once you go on the difficult journey of wrestling and struggling with God and the Bible, you can begin to imagine what it might look like to invite your students on this same journey.

THE WEEK WE ALL FEAR

After you've modeled this journey to your students, you must recognize that you can't force them into this same struggle, just like nobody could have forced you into it. But you can create environments for students to enter into this struggle when they're ready.

Several years ago, two students from a local high school passed away during the same week. One, a girl named Alyssa, passed away after a long battle with cancer. The other, Ryan, was a hockey player who died in his sleep because of an undiagnosed heart condition. These two deaths in the span of one week pushed many in our community into a state of numbness. The students at this high school were experiencing shock and trauma.

Alyssa was a member of our church and youth group, and we did everything we could to care for her family and friends. Ryan was an exceptional and well-known athlete, and his passing impacted many in our community who had not even met him. Our staff spent time at the local school meeting with students and teachers, and tried to be present to the pain of anyone who needed support.

By the end of that week, our team had lingering questions about what to do at our normal youth group gathering the following Sunday night. Should we continue with the program and experience we already had planned? Do we cancel everything and create space for our students to process what happened? Is some sort of hybrid possible?

Are we allowed to have fun? How do we honor Alyssa, Ryan, and their friends and families? How do we respect those who may not have been directly impacted by their deaths? What do our volunteers need from us to be prepared to step into this space? How on earth should we talk to parents about any of this?

We did our best with the intuition and experience we had, and I'm sure it was all handled quite imperfectly. However, we tried to create space for the kind of struggle and wrestling the Bible models for us.

Based on what I learned from this and other experiences with loss, here are some suggestions for engaging a community of students and Scripture in these moments as ministry leaders with honesty, lament, and hope:

1. *Help students name and understand what is true.*

   In this situation, we began our large group gathering by simply stating the fact that both Alyssa and Ryan had died. We intentionally chose to say "died" instead of "passed away," because we wanted to do everything we could to avoid glossing over the reality of what had happened. I remember after saying the word, "died," I heard several students burst into tears from where they were sitting. It was as if they just needed someone to tell them again that this was true.

2. *Validate everything that our students and volunteers might be experiencing and feeling.*

   They may not have the tools or maturity to do so on their own, and if they do, they may worry that how they're really feeling isn't "youth group appropriate." I remember listing a full range of possible responses and emotions, not in a prescriptive way, but in a descriptive way, doing my best to communicate that any response and emotion in this situation is natural and okay, and that nobody needs to pretend to feel any differently than they really do.

3. *Be personally vulnerable.*

Again, this is why entering into wrestling and struggle in your own life is so important. Our young people need us to guide them through it, which means we need to lead the way. I remember saying, "I knew Alyssa and I know her family. I never had the chance to meet Ryan, but I graduated from the high school where he was a student and I know so many students and teachers from that school who knew Ryan well. I am absolutely heartbroken, and I am absolutely pissed off that this happened."

4. *Invite students into seeing the Bible as a struggle and wrestling match between humans and the divine.*

The temptation in these moments is to offer hope through biblical promises. However, we can offer a greater and more tangible sense of hope to our students, not through biblical promises that may gloss over the pain of the moment, but through "biblical empathy." By biblical empathy, I mean sharing the raw pain, suffering, struggle, and wrestling that we find in the Bible. Rather than telling students, "God works all things together for the good of those who love him" (Romans 8:28 NIV), tell your students that Jesus questioned God and felt abandoned and forsaken at the moment of his death, that Jacob was a mixed-up guy who lived a mixed-up life but had the courage to wrestle with God all night. Or share how one of the most repeated questions in the psalms is "How long, Lord?" and tell them about Lamentations.

5. **Tell students that the Christian faith is big enough for the pain they're experiencing and that God can handle their audacity and struggle.**

Tell them that, like Jacob, they may feel like running from God for a while, but eventually those same feelings might lead them to question, doubt, rage, and wrestle with God. Tell students that this is part of what it means to be a human being and that God will engage with them in their struggle. Encourage them to be real about how they're feeling with God; that no language, expression, or emotion is inappropriate if it's how they truly feel. This is why we have the practice of lament in the biblical and ongoing Christian tradition—to validate our honesty before God when it's not praise or thanksgiving.

6. **Give students a release valve.**

Here's another way of saying this: If there ever *should* be pizza at youth group, it should be at a gathering where you're struggling and wrestling. If you have the courage to create this sort of environment with your students, it's important that you offer them a way "out" of the environment before they go home. This doesn't mean that you tie a bow on the message or try to resolve everything during small groups. It means that you remind students of the absurdity and complexity of life by showing them how to move out of intense conversations and into constructive ways of using their energy and enjoying one another's company. This might mean ordering pizza and having root beer floats, an impromptu dance party, or an epic four-square battle that lasts well beyond the "end time" of your youth group. Some of the most meaningful interactions I've had with students have been when we've allowed ourselves a few moments of enjoyment in the shadow of immense pain.

These moments and conversations are the kind we pray we never have to experience with our students, for whom we care so much. However, these are also the moments that can have the most dramatic and positive impact in the lives of young people. It's not a matter of *if* you will have the opportunity to struggle and wrestle with God and the Bible with your students, but *when*. May we have the courage, freedom, and audacity to do so.

TRY THIS ... IN YOUR LIFE:

- Spend some time with the questions listed earlier in this chapter regarding your own interior work with struggle. Regardless of how you answer the questions, consider finding a good friend, or perhaps a therapist or counselor, to help you process your reactions.

- Find a separate journal to begin recording your own laments, complaints, or struggles with God. Pray through this journal on a regular basis.

- Interview an older member of your congregation. Ask him or her about some of their greatest experiences of struggle and pain, and how this impacted how they read the Bible.

- If you don't experience a need or desire to struggle and wrestle with God, ask God if there are any areas of your life where God desires to struggle and wrestle with you.

- Begin reading a psalm before or after every meal. Take note of how many of them convey a tone of struggle or lament.

TRY THIS ... IN YOUR MINISTRY:

- Pay attention to the lyrics of the music you play and invite students to sing during worship times. Try to include more songs that leave questions unanswered and tap into experiences of raw struggle and wrestling.

- Find appropriate times and ways to share some of your darkest moments of faith, and what it looked like for you to wrestle with God.

- Pay attention to what is going on in the news. It's likely your students are more impacted by tragedy than you might think. Leverage these events as opportunities to invite your students into honest dialogue about life and faith. Read and pray psalms of lament in response to injustice in the world and in your local community.

- Lead a study or series on the sections of the Bible that include people arguing, struggling, or wrestling with God.

- When you're teaching or reading the Bible with students, find ways to humanize the characters in the stories. Even if some of your comments are speculative, invite students to consider the real faith struggles of the real people included in the Bible. Some questions to ask might include, "I wonder how they were feeling when this happened?" or, "I wonder what question they had for God?"

8

A PRAYER BOOK

IS THE BIBLE ONLY GOD'S WORD TO US, OR ALSO OUR WORDS TO GOD?

Jesus was praying in a certain place. When he finished, one of his disciples said, "Lord, teach us to pray, just as John taught his disciples."

LUKE 11:1

CLOSING IN PRAYER

It was the last day of Bible study for the summer, and I was exhausted.

It had been an extraordinarily challenging school year with our high school students and volunteers. I was running on fumes. In addition to the fatigue I was experiencing near the end of the marathon that was our youth ministry calendar year, I had returned home the night before from Israel, where I had led a study tour with a group of college students. I'd spent the previous two weeks hiking, sweating, teaching, and sharing insight from sunup to sundown. Introducing young people to the land of the Bible was an unbelievable honor and privilege, but I was jet-lagged, dehydrated, and felt like I hadn't seen my wife in years. Truth be told, I had done so much teaching in the past two weeks that I wasn't feeling too excited to share more "biblical insight" with anyone for a while.

Despite my best intentions, I hadn't prepared anything for our last summer Bible study before I left for Israel. I told myself I'd have time to prepare during the long flight home, but then the unimaginable happened: I had three empty seats between me and the window, and I slept across them the entire flight from Tel Aviv to Chicago. Even so, I was still exhausted and feeling slightly overwhelmed about the evening.

In a few hours, I would lead our last Bible study of the summer, and I still didn't have a plan. Well, that's not entirely true. I knew we were going to have ice cream sundaes at the end of the night. The feelings of insecurity about our gathering led me to quickly check our program budget to see if I had enough money left to order pizza. I also did a quick online search to see if there was any new, hip, and free youth group video curriculum that had been released in the previous two weeks.

I was getting desperate. We were supposed to be doing a study on prayer, but I just wasn't feeling it. There was a stack of open commentaries and a list of Bible verses on my desk. I wasn't short on information, but I felt like I had nothing to say.

And while I know everyone's circumstances are different, I am certain that I'm not the only youth worker who has experienced the midafternoon terror of not having a clear plan for that evening, or feeling like you're so tired that you have nothing helpful to offer. I can't be the only person who has looked at the clock and thought, "One minute closer to youth group, and one minute closer to me finding a new job if I don't come up with something."

I decided to stop hastily flipping books open, trying to find the insight that would provoke curiosity and provide energy for the evening, and instead began re-reading my notes and journal from my time in Israel. I was reminded that just a few days earlier, our group had made the difficult climb to the top of Mount Arbel together and spent some time overlooking the Sea of Galilee. Mount Arbel is near the western shore of the Sea of Galilee between Tiberius and Capernaum. Several steep cliffs offer breathtaking views of the entire region.

Mark 6:45-56 tells us that after a day of teaching (and feeding five thousand people), Jesus sends his disciples ahead of him on the Sea of Galilee and then climbs a mountain to pray. Later, he sees them struggling on the water and goes to help. Mt. Arbel is one of the places of prayer and solitude Jesus may have sought out in this story, or in any of the stories in the Gospels where Jesus retreats to pray while in the Galilee region.

I have climbed Mt. Arbel several times with groups, and one of the impulses that people experience once we reach the top is to offer gratitude and prayer. It's a difficult and dangerous enough climb that people literally want to express, "Thank God we made it! Thank God it's over." The instinct to pray together after reaching the top is a great lead-in to the content I usually teach at that location regarding Jesus and prayer.

After that first quick prayer, we got out our maps and oriented ourselves to the geography of our location. I pointed out some interesting sights around the Sea of Galilee that we could see uniquely from our elevation, and we read through some of the stories in the Gospels when Jesus left the crowds behind to experience quiet, solitude, and prayer.

At the end of our group discussion, I asked if anyone would like to pray for our group, since we just spent so much time talking about Jesus and prayer, and because we now had to make the risky descent down Mt. Arbel. One of the students asked if instead of "closing our time together in prayer," we could instead spend a few more minutes on top of the mountain while she led us through the practice of *lectio divina*.

This was an excellent idea, and the kind of excellent idea

that left me feeling embarrassed as a pastor, teacher, and guide. Instead of climbing a mountain and talking about prayer together, the idea of *actually praying* in a place where Jesus prayed is something I should have considered. What I was treating as a bookend to our experience, she was elevating as the main point. So, this student explained the practice, which was new for many in our group, and we clumsily worked through *lectio divina* together.

Praying this way was a profound experience. At the end of the trip, many of our participants pointed to that moment as a highlight.

A DIVINE IDEA

If you're not familiar with *lectio divina* (pronounced LEX-ee-oh div-EEHN-ah), it's a Latin phrase that literally means "Divine Reading," and is a traditional Benedictine practice that beautifully blurs the line between prayer and Scripture reading. This practice usually involves inviting a group into a silent and meditative posture while a passage of Scripture is read aloud slowly. The passage is usually read multiple times, with a period of silence between each reading. Any passage of Scripture will work for this practice, but generally a shorter passage works better (for example, a parable, a story from the Gospels, or a psalm).

As the verses are read, participants do their best to clear their minds and to allow the words to "fall over" them. Often, the goal is to listen for a word or phrase, either from the passage itself or one that is provoked by the passage, that rises to the surface in the individual's heart or mind.

After the text is read several times, more time and space is usually offered for participants to reflect on their one word or phrase. In many cases, individuals will share their word or phrase with the rest of the group. For everyone participating, the active listening and sharing of this practice is meant to be an exercise in non-judgment, as we learn to listen without judging our thoughts, and as we learn not to judge what is shared by others in the group.

All of this is meant to invite participants into communion with God and one another, and to experience the Bible not as a text out of which we derive meaning, but as the Living Word still speaking to each of us.

The practice of *lectio divina* invites participants to trust that the word or phrase they hear during this practice is coming from deep within them, and is in some way the Word of God spoken to them and to the community. In this practice, the Bible becomes a book of prayers to be heard and prayed in our relationship with God and one another.

FROM INSIGHT TO PRAYER

Before the Israel trip, I had engaged in *lectio divina* countless times, most often with mixed results. On occasion, I felt like what I was hearing came from a divine source beyond its being a passage of sacred Scripture— that there was in fact something I was hearing from God in that moment. There also were many times when, as I was doing my best to sit in silence and allow the Scripture reading to fall upon me, my mind and heart were constantly bouncing from my to-do list, to my bottomless email inbox, to the Detroit Tigers game the night before, to trying to stay awake.

That last one was a major point of insecurity for me. I was terrified of the embarrassment that would come from falling asleep in a group of colleagues and uber-spiritual people as we tried to listen for the voice of God.

I had always left engaging in this practice feeling like I was less spiritual than the others I had been with, and that maybe someday I might desire to participate in the same way they did.

But there were also times that I wanted to interrupt this practice and just yell, "BORING!" This, obviously, says more about my immaturity than it does about the practice itself.

Regardless of my response, I had always left engaging in this practice feeling like I was less spiritual than the others I had been with, and that maybe someday I might desire to participate in the same way they did. But somehow it seemed beyond me.

But during the previous two weeks in Israel, something changed. Maybe it was the beautiful view of the Sea of Galilee from Mt. Arbel, maybe it was a sign of the growing relationships that are uniquely forged during a trip like this, or maybe it was a moment of spiritual transition for me. Whatever it was, our group practice of *lectio* under the afternoon sun changed me, and it gave me a more expansive view of what the Bible is and how we can interact with it.

For years I had known what the Bible says about itself: It is living, God-breathed, and sharper than a sword (2 Timothy 3:16, Hebrews 4:12). But all of these self-descriptions the Bible offers felt more like creative literary devices than something I experienced as concretely true. Until that moment on Mt. Arbel. And a few days later, while I didn't yet know that it had set me on a new spiritual trajectory, I did sense that that sacred moment was going to bail me out of not knowing what to do for our last summer Bible study.

"Every scripture is inspired by God and is useful for teaching, for showing mistakes, for correcting, and for training character, so that the person who belongs to God can be equipped to do everything that is good."

2 TIMOTHY 3:16-17

"God's word is living, active, and sharper than any two-edged sword. It penetrates to the point that it separates the soul from the spirit and the joints from the marrow. It's able to judge the heart's thoughts and intentions. No creature is hidden from it, but rather everything is naked and exposed to the eyes of the one to whom we have to give an answer."

HEBREWS 4:12-13

A few weeks earlier, I would have avoided practicing *lectio divina* for myself, and now I was going to try to get a bunch of teenagers to sit in extended silence and listen for the voice of God. My anxiety quickly pivoted from not having a study prepared to whether or not this was a practice our students were ready for.

MODERN RESEARCH AND ANCIENT WISDOM

Research conducted by the Fuller Youth Institute through both *Sticky Faith* and *Growing Young* projects (see fulleryouthinstitute.org) overwhelmingly points to the role and value of spiritual practices in the spiritual formation of adolescents and emerging adults. While much of our time and energy as youth workers is often spent introducing and explaining the Bible to young people, the research indicates that our sermons, lessons, and Bible studies may not have the sort of impact we think. At the very least, the results are likely disproportionate to the time and energy given to these sorts of activities.

To be clear, I'm not questioning whether or not sermons or Bible studies have value, I'm only asking us to consider whether or not there are other ways we as youth workers could expose our students to the Bible that may be equally, if not more, formative.

This modern research about the spiritual formation of young people actually isn't so modern—it validates the way early Christians experienced the Bible, which was the same as the Jewish people during the Second Temple period in which Jesus lived. Most people during this time period were illiterate, and if they could read, they didn't have access to the scriptures. It's likely a community or a town may have had only one copy of only parts of the books that make up what we know as the Bible. Because of this, the Bible wasn't individually studied or used to provide support for long sermons. Instead, the Bible often was sung and recited as part of individual, familial, and communal prayer experiences.

The Bible was the prayer book of the people.

The first followers of Jesus had God's words on their lips as they spoke to God in prayer, and it was God's word in their ears as they listened to God in prayer.

From what we know, the Jewish people during the Second Temple period, as well as the earliest Jewish followers of Jesus, made the words of Deuteronomy 6 a primary part of their spiritual and religious lives:

> Hear, O Israel: The LORD our God, the LORD is one. Love the LORD your God with all your heart and with all your soul and with all your strength. These commandments that I give you today are to be on your hearts. Impress them on your children. Talk about them when you sit at home and when you walk along the road, when you lie down and when you get up. Tie them as symbols on your hands and bind them on your foreheads. Write them on the doorframes of your houses and on your gates.

DEUTERONOMY 6:4-9, NIV

This recitation is known as the "Shema," which is the first Hebrew word of the passage, meaning "listen" or "hear." This text was recited not just as a reminder or creed, but as a prayer of devotion every morning and evening, because the passage says you should "talk about them ... when you lie down and when you get up."

In Matthew 22, when someone asks Jesus, "What is the greatest commandment?", he responds by quoting this passage, as if to say, "The greatest commandment is also the greatest prayer." Praying God's words back to God was the most natural thing in the world. On a practical level, it makes sense. Why would I pray my own words when I can pray God's words?

This reality gives us a greater window into how reading the Bible as a prayer book can actually work. Trusting that the words of Scripture are somehow the words of God, and that God is still speaking through these words, moves us from a didactic and educational reading of the Bible into an experiential and mystical reading of the Bible.

Praying God's words back to God was the most natural thing in the world.

Our students are immersed in a culture filled with noise, screens, and busyness, where silence and solitude are both a struggle and a luxury. We mostly agree that this is a problem, but I'm not sure if more information *about* God is the solution. Our students are desperate for spiritual experiences and divine encounters, and I wholeheartedly believe Christianity already has everything we need within our tradition to unlock this reality for our young people. What if God became less of an idea to be understood and more of an experience to be had? As youth workers, our responsibility is to introduce the Bible to our students in such a way that it can facilitate these encounters.

This can be a difficult reality for us to navigate in our youth groups.

LESS TALKING AND MORE PRAYING

During college, I was a volunteer small group leader in my church. A group of rowdy guys from a local high school showed up at my house every Wednesday night. We'd eat food together, watch *The Best of Will Ferrell* on DVD, and every week we studied the Bible. The core group of guys in this gathering all loved learning about the Bible, they loved the church we attended, and they all ran cross country. On a regular basis, they brought other guys from their cross-country team to join us for small group.

Early on, the guys started bringing Chad along.

Chad naturally fit in, he was fun, and he was a really bright guy. He was always interested in our conversations, and he enjoyed learning about Jesus and the Bible. But I never really knew what he believed, where he stood with God, or what his faith was all about. I was a student in Bible college, so we had serious Bible studies every Wednesday night. On one particular Wednesday in the summer of 2003, we were studying Luke 11, where Jesus teaches his disciples about prayer. We began with Luke 11:1, which says:

> "One day Jesus was praying in a certain place. When he finished, one of his disciples said to him, 'Lord, teach us to pray, just as John taught his disciples.'"

In response to this question, Jesus offers what is considered Luke's version of "The Lord's Prayer." Together, we discussed how this prayer reveals the things that were most important to Jesus, and why those things should be important to us and be the kinds of things we should pray about.

Jesus told them, "When you pray, say:
'Father, uphold the holiness of your name.
Bring in your kingdom.
Give us the bread we need for today.
Forgive us our sins,
for we also forgive everyone who has wronged us.
And don't lead us into temptation.'"

LUKE 11:2-4

I actually think it was one of the best Bible studies I'd ever led. Seriously, to this day, I'd say it was a "top five" teaching moment. We finished the study, and as the guys started to leave, Chad kind of just kept hanging around. After some small talk, he asked if we could go in another room where my roommates wouldn't disturb us. He looked terrified.

We went in another room and sat down in two chairs across from each other.

I asked, "What's up, Chad?"

And he said, "I really liked your Bible study tonight. I learned a lot."

"Thanks."

"Can I ask you a question?"

"Of course."

"Can you teach me how to pray?"

"Well, Chad, we just spent an hour talking about that," I said. "I thought you said you learned a lot during my Bible study."

I'll never forget this moment, because Chad looked me in the eyes and said, "Well, I did learn a lot about prayer. But I've never actually prayed before, and I'm wondering if you could help me do it."

That night Chad prayed for the first time. I prayed, and then he prayed, and then we prayed together.

After we prayed, Chad asked me a few more questions. Then he thanked me, gave me a hug, and left my house.

I went in my room, closed the door, and wept. It was a beautiful moment, and it was such a gift from God. I was so grateful. But I also felt embarrassed, and a little ashamed.

I had just led an hour-long Bible study with a group of high school guys on Luke 11 that started with Jesus' disciples saying, "Teach us to pray," and when we were finished with our study, Chad still asked the same question as Jesus' disciples.

I missed the point of the passage.

But Chad didn't.

Chad didn't show up looking for more information about his faith. He was looking for a chance to *do something* about whatever faith he had, to take action, to put it into practice. And he was looking for someone to do it with him—not just to tell him how or to do it for him, but to show him and do it with him.

How many sermons or lessons about prayer have our students heard in their lives? Depending on the student, probably a lot. Unfortunately, this number is probably much larger than the amount of times we have actually prayed with any of those students. When the Bible remains only a source of information, rather than an experience to be practiced or a prayer to be prayed, we miss out on inviting students into one of the most effective paths of spiritual formation.

PUTTING IT INTO PRACTICE: PRAYING WITH SCRIPTURE TOGETHER

Back to the evening when I hadn't prepared in advance for Summer Bible Study: When we began our gathering, I explained that we were going to be doing something a little different and asked everyone if they were up for trying an experiment. They knew something was up from the moment they arrived, because we had removed all of the chairs from the room.

Here's the framing and instructions we gave for the experience before we tried *lectio divina* with our youth group:

1. Spread out around the room, find your own space, and sit on the carpet.

2. Swing your arms and legs around, like making a "snow angel" on the floor. If you're able to touch anyone else, you are too close to another person and need to find a new space.

3. Lie on the ground and close your eyes. We're going to spend nearly a half hour on the floor, so get comfortable.

4. You don't have to do everything I'm asking, and it's fine if you fall asleep, but please avoid distracting any of the people around you.

5. I'm giving you a couple of minutes to try to clear your minds and to take deep breaths.

6. What we're about to experience is an ancient practice called *lectio divina*. I'm going to read a passage to you several times, and the invitation is just to listen. Pay attention to a word or phrase from the passage that leaves an impression on you, or listen for anything else that might come to your heart during this time.

And then we did it.

For nearly thirty minutes, one hundred high school students laid on the floor of our student room in silence while we listened to the Bible and waited in silence.

After reading the passage several times, I invited them to remain in silence while they sat up, stretched, and came to the center of the room where we gathered in a circle. I then invited them to share the word or phrase that they heard, and also told them if they didn't want to say anything because it was private or they hadn't heard anything or they had fallen asleep, they could say, "Pass," and that was fine, too. The person sitting on my left started, then we moved around the circle. Some students shared a word, some a phrase, and some a sentence. Nobody tried to explain or qualify anything. They just shared what they heard.

Every student shared something.

Nobody said, "Pass."

After we had completed our circle, I invited students to share what the experience felt like to them. The first student to speak was the one I was most concerned about when I was imagining all that could go wrong if we tried this practice together.

She said, "This is the coolest thing we've ever done at youth group."

Many of the students nodded in agreement. It became clear to me that we had entered into sacred space together, and that nobody wanted to leave this space. After a bit more conversation, I realized that I was going to have to be the one to crack a joke at the appropriate time so that I could explain there were ice cream sundaes waiting for us in another room.

This experience came nearly ten years after I began my journey with the Bible, and I had been leading this high school ministry long enough to have shaped a culture of Bible reading and teaching. The Bible had become a number of things to us during the journey, but in this moment, perhaps for the first time, it became our prayer book. Our engagement with the Bible moved from "discipline" to "practice," and we had a group of witnesses to the reality that God has spoken and is still speaking, and that we have the ability to listen in deep and meaningful ways. For many of our students that evening, both God and the Bible moved from abstract concepts to concrete realities—from information to understand to encounters to be experienced.

While this was deeply satisfying, it also left us wanting more.

So we tried to experience more together.

The following spring break a group of us went on a service trip to the Gulf Coast to serve those who were still rebuilding their lives and homes years after Hurricane Katrina. It was tradition on this trip for our team to provide a devotional guide for the week. Usually this comprised a few Scripture passages and some guiding questions for students and leaders to engage on their own before breakfast. But on this trip, we scrapped the "morning devotions" and made our own fixed-hour prayer guide. We loosely modeled our guide after the ancient Christian tradition of praying the scriptures at specific times through each 24-hour cycle.

Instead of giving our students Bible verses to read in the

morning, we assigned Scripture to specific times throughout the day, and instructed our leaders that no matter what their group of students was doing at those times, they needed to stop as a group and read and listen to the Scripture verses assigned to that hour. They were free to have a discussion afterwards, but we provided no guiding questions that would imply prescribed answers or behaviors. We simply wanted students and leaders to stop working and pray the scriptures together at set times throughout the day.

This was met with some resistance at first among our veteran leaders, because the normal routine of morning devotions held significant value for them, and because they felt inconvenienced about pulling off the side of the road or getting a team of students off of the roof in the middle of shingling a house so they could pray at a specific time. But by the end of the week, the rhythm of working, resting, praying the scriptures, and listening had become one of the highlights of the experience for many students and leaders. During our debriefing conversations in the weeks and months following the trip, it was these moments that students pointed to when they described hearing from God or something about our experience together shaping their faith in a new way.

Years ago, I would have scoffed at the idea of inviting students into reading the Bible as a prayer book, but every time I have had the imagination to believe that our students desire more, and are capable of handling more than we often give them credit, I've never been disappointed.

And whenever we've tried more, it's always left us wanting more.

And I bet you and your students are looking for more as well.

TRY THIS ... IN YOUR LIFE:

- For a season, consider replacing your "personal prayers" with praying Scripture. Find a guide for using *The Book of Common Prayer* or some modified version of it. I highly recommend *The Divine Hours* series by the late Phyllis Tickle.

- Reflect on a biblical character or story with which you've resonated, and read the related Scripture as a practice of prayer.

- Do some online research on the practice of *lectio divina*, and find a colleague or fellow youth worker to experiment with the practice with you.

- Read selected passages of Scripture repetitively, in the posture of prayer. Try reading a passage five times, with a period of one to two minutes of silence between each reading.

- Visit a local synagogue, or a church from a more liturgical Christian tradition, and make note of how Scripture is used as a form of prayer in their services. If you're visiting a synagogue, I'd recommend calling ahead to tell them you're coming and why. They'll be delighted to have you.

TRY THIS ... IN YOUR MINISTRY:

- For a season, any time during your youth group gathering that you would have offered an improvised prayer, consider replacing it with praying a psalm or some other passage of Scripture that fits the tone or theme of the evening.

- If your youth group sings together, consider introducing Scripture readings or prayers from Scripture for your group to say together in between songs.

- As mentioned in chapter 7, use psalms of lament from the Bible to help students learn to wrestle with God in prayer. Psalms can also be used as language for prayers of gratitude, wonder, or petition. Old Testament scholar and Fuller professor John Goldingay calls the psalms "a collection of 150 examples of the things you can say to God."[1] Try offering the psalms this way to students.

- Consider a series or season where you're spending more time apprenticing your students and volunteers in the practice of prayer and Bible reading, rather than giving them information or sermons about prayer.

---

1 John Goldingay with Jesse Oakes, "A book we read that also reads us: A conversation about the psalms with Dr. John Goldingay," Fuller Youth Institute, https://fulleryouthinstitute.org/articles/a-book-we-read-that-also-reads-us.

- Do a study on the prayers that biblical characters or other followers of Jesus have prayed throughout history (e.g., David, Mary, Jesus, Paul, Oscar Romero, Mother Teresa, Martin Luther King, Jr.), and invite your youth group to pray these prayers together.

- Consider practicing *lectio divina*, or a modified version of it, with your students. Don't feel like you have to "go for it" right away. Even five or ten minutes could be transformative for your students.

- Pray the Lord's Prayer regularly for a season, perhaps learning a version of the prayer together that feels like modern language, in whatever language your students know best. Try using the Lord's Prayer as a "starter prayer" for students' own prayers, making each phrase a prompt and allowing students to speak or write their own prayers while you pause before going on to the next phrase.

CONCLUSION

A JOURNEY TO CONTINUE

Blessed are those whose strength is in you, whose hearts are set on pilgrimage.

PSALM 84:5, NIV

INNOCENCE LOST

Shortly after the first time I visited church as a high school senior, I attended a "town hall" style meeting led by several elders and staff members from my new church. The church was considering changing its bylaws and doctrinal statement regarding a specific issue, and the leadership of the community wanted to hear feedback from members before moving forward.

At the beginning of the meeting, two staff members gave short presentations.

The first offered an argument for one side of the issue. This person was funny, used creative slides, and referenced plenty of Bible verses that seemed to make the argument clear.

The second offered an argument for the other side of the issue. This person was also funny, used creative slides, and referenced plenty of Bible verses that made the argument clear.

Both of these individuals spoke kindly of one another and of the opposing view during their presentation, but each was clearly advocating for one specific response to the issue.

I remember being wide-eyed, astonished, and impressed after each of the presentations and the dialogue that took place between them. I was so new to the Bible and to Christianity that I had never experienced something like this before. How could it be that there were Bible verses that seemed to clearly support differing sides of the same issue? How could it be that two people who had opposing opinions could present arguments with so much kindness and generosity toward one another?

But then the tone of the meeting changed.

Members of the congregation were invited to ask questions and offer comments at one of several microphones placed around the sanctuary. Once the invitation was made clear, lines formed behind each microphone. Everyone in line held a Bible. Most of the people didn't have questions; they only offered comments. With each person who shared, the tone became more intense, and some of the congregants began to verbally attack the motives of the staff members who had presented.

The intensity climaxed when two members of the community were each standing at different microphones, jamming their pointed fingers onto the pages of their open Bibles, and yelling as they read their respective passage of Scripture at one another.

The venom in the room caused me to feel ill.

It was enough to make me consider not returning to the church—a church with which I had so quickly fallen in love.

In the many years that have passed since this experience, I've spent a lot of time reflecting on what happened, why it happened, and what we all could learn from it. I've been able to see that for most of the people in attendance that night, there was much more going on in the conversation than I realized at the time.

The people in this community, who deeply loved both the

Bible and our church, weren't just concerned about the specific issue at hand. They were concerned that the Bible wasn't being taken seriously. As both sides used the Bible to support their arguments, tension built, and the reflexive way to resolve that tension was for each side to propose that the Bible wasn't being taken seriously by the opposite group. Allowing two staff members to present two opposing views of the issue with the support of passages from the Bible only fueled the fire, because this approach solidified the idea that only one of two possibilities was accurate, true, and faithful.

Looking back, we didn't actually need someone to answer, "What does the Bible say?" about the topic. Most everyone in attendance already had their Bible verses locked and loaded when they arrived.

We didn't even need someone to answer, "What is the Bible?" Most everyone in attendance was certain they were standing upon the inspired, infallible, and inerrant Word of God.

What we needed was someone to show us a map.

We needed someone to help us see that we must consider *how* we read the Bible, as a precursor to discussing *what* we think the Bible is saying.

Bible scholar Justo González says this about reading Scripture: "The landscape is the same for all of us. Yet each one sees it from a different perspective, and will thus describe it differently.["1] Members of our church were looking at the same landscape, but from different angles, altitudes, and lighting. Perhaps it could have changed everything if someone had shown us that the primary point of conflict during this meeting wasn't the actual issue we were debating. Instead, the conflict arose because we were all occupying different locations on a map without the ability to recognize that the map itself was bigger than any of our positions.

We may not have all come to agreement that evening, but a greater level of collective awareness would have changed the tone of the conversation and our ability to see a way forward together.

I've become more and more convinced that how we practice reading the Bible may be just as important as what we believe about the Bible.

WHERE DO WE GROW FROM HERE?

Our students need us to help them experience a broad and generous perspective of the Bible.

---

1 Justo Gonzalez, *Santa Biblia: The Bible through Hispanic Eyes (Nashville: Abingdon Press,* 1996). See also fullerstudio.fuller.edu/our-culturally-shaped-lenses/

Our students need us to inspire them with an imagination and appreciation for an ever-expanding map of how we read the Bible.

In this book, I've offered various approaches for how we might go about reading and understanding Scripture. But maybe at this point you're asking the questions:

Where do I start?

What place on the map should I call home first?

Are these the only ways to read the Bible, or are there more?

Here are three possible ways forward that I think will be helpful as you sort through these questions.

1. LET JESUS BE YOUR GUIDE

First, let Jesus be your guide on this journey. If what I've tried to offer us is an imagination for a broader map of how we read the Bible, I want to propose that Jesus can be our guide to that map (and all that may be beyond it). If you don't know where to start, start with Jesus.

A broad reading of the Gospels reveals that Jesus himself read the Bible in all of the ways we've discussed in this book (and likely many more) during his life and ministry. With that in mind, ask yourself these questions as you think about what it might look like to inhabit each unique location on the map of how we read the Bible:

- What was Jesus' personal relationship with the Bible?

- Which commands did Jesus live out? Which ones did he reinterpret (or even break)?

- How did the physicality of the Bible's contexts impact Jesus?

- What did Jesus' "way" look like in practice?

- How did Jesus find his place in the story?

- What questions did Jesus ask?

- In what ways did Jesus wrestle with God?

- Which scriptures did Jesus pray?

Jesus had a unique and beautiful perspective on and interaction with the biblical texts. And while I don't want to recommend that trying to copy Jesus in everything is the answer (or even possible), there might be something helpful for us in trying to emulate Jesus' relationship with the Bible as we sort through the implications of this book for our lives and for our students.

For example, what do we do with the fact that Jesus seemed to be more familiar with, and likely even favored, some parts of the Bible over others? He gives people permission to break commandments that are clearly prescribed by the Torah, and offers redefinition to other commandments. Jesus often demands spiritual and scriptural conversations to be sorted out in the midst of concrete, flesh-and-blood, practical issues of life. Jesus pushes forward the unfolding story of who God is and what it means to be made in God's image. Jesus' questions challenge all systems and authorities, and the audacity with which he wrestles with God could be considered offensive even to some of the prophets. Jesus' use of the Bible in prayer happened outside of the Temple and the synagogue, and not always at the prescribed times or in the usual ways.

So, consider starting with Jesus and let him be your guide as you read. But don't get too comfortable, because Jesus will likely lead you into uncharted territory—perhaps way off the map.

2. CHART YOUR COURSE

Second, chart your course for this journey. While some trips are best experienced unplanned, and God often works in ways outside of the methods we imagine or expect, I highly recommend making an intentional plan for how to move through different ways of engaging the Bible with your students. In fact, I think the ways we read the Bible that are described in this book could help us to reimagine, or perhaps refine, what a curriculum scope and sequence could look like in our ministries.

Here's what I mean:

In chapter 3 I mentioned that our student ministries team had spent months trying to put together a meticulous and seamless curriculum scope and sequence beginning in our nursery and concluding with post-high school students. I remember our group meeting for hours at a time, hiding from distractions in a grungy upstairs storage room at our church. We sat on the floor and sketched on large pieces of paper and a small whiteboard. We desperately wanted to make sure that the young people who were growing up in our church's kids and student ministries would be exposed to every part of the Bible at least once.

We had many arguments about which parts of the Bible were most age-appropriate for different groups, and every time we thought we were close to having a plan, someone on our team would share a consideration that compelled us to go back to the drawing board.

Eventually, we ended up with a chart composed of multiple columns. One column named the specific birth through post-high school ministry programs that were offered in our community. In our context, these programs were distinguished by age and/or grade in school. Another column listed the unique developmental stages that existed within each of those program and age groups. For example, the children who participated in our preschool ministry would be in different developmental stages than the students in our high school ministry. We also included some distinguishing information about each developmental stage that might impact what we taught. Another column included calendars of the school year with specific sections of the Bible assigned to each date on the calendar. (This is how I ended up trying to eat a scroll, as I mentioned in chapter 3. During the first cycle of this curriculum scope and sequence, I was assigned to teach on Ezekiel during the month of March.) By the time we finished, our chart needed a bigger piece of paper than our printer could handle, and the font was obnoxiously small. But we had completed the tedious and important work of intentionally charting a course for the ways in which we would engage the Bible with our students.

This was an ambitious and difficult task fueled by genuine motives to help students grow, and it was worth every minute of the work. Over ten years later, the current ministry leaders at the church are still working from an evolving version of this plan. It brings me so much joy to know that the young people in this community have been on an intentional journey with the Bible for over a decade.

While I'm proud of the work we accomplished, if I had to do this process again I would do it completely differently. Here's why:

As we charted this course, we focused solely on the "what" of the Bible. We argued and deliberated about which ministry should be teaching "what" part of the Bible, and when they might be doing that. And we accomplished our goal, because nearly all of the Bible was accounted for on our chart.

However, we spent almost no time charting a course for "how" we were going to read the Bible with our students.

Looking back, rather than only assigning books and sections of the Bible to specific programs and grade levels, I wonder how it would have been different if we had correlated age-appropriate methods and practices for how we read the Bible to each of our ministry programs.

While I think that course we charted was effective, I wish we had asked,

"Have our students learned how to read the Bible as story?"

And

"Have our students gained experience in praying the words of the Bible?"

And

"Do our students have a greater sense of discerning what the Bible is asking of them?"

And

"Are our students comfortable with reading the Bible on their own?"

Rather than only asking,

"Did our students spend enough time learning from the book of Exodus?"

And

"Was it too much for our students that we tried to cram all the Minor Prophets into a six-week series during Lent?

And

"Do our students understand the message of the book of Romans?"

And

"Have our students mastered this content?"

I wish we had charted a course centered on the method rather than the message alone, so our students would be better equipped to engage the message for the rest of their lives.

And you have the opportunity to chart this course for your students.

Whether it's the eight ways I've described regarding how we read the Bible, a shorter list, or your version of an expanding map, I recommend that you find your equivalent of the grungy upstairs room of our church. Bring some of your colleagues, volunteers, and students, and some large pieces of paper. Begin sketching what it might look like for different age groups in your community to engage these ways of reading the Bible. Think both about the *what* and the *how*.

> *I wish we had charted a course centered on the method rather than the message alone, so our students would be better equipped to engage the message for the rest of their lives.*

While I think each location on the map can be hospitable for all ages, I don't think it's an accident that my journey evolved in this order as I grew older, and also grew deeper in my faith. There is some merit to more strongly correlating approaches from earlier chapters of this book with younger children or students, or with those new to the faith, and to move from there. For example, elementary school kids may benefit from a little more time spent reading the Bible as book, commands, or story, while high school students who may have been part of your community for most of their lives might be desperate for someone to help them read the Bible as a book of questions, prayers, or as a wrestling match. Again, what I've offered is a description of one way to chart the course based on my own journey. I am not necessarily prescribing that you chart the exact course in this exact order for your life or for your students.

3. KEEP GOING

Third, keep going on this journey of engaging the Bible.

If we want to keep growing, we have to keep going.

Our personal practices for how we read the Bible or engage it with our students can become static or stale. When they do, what can help us get out of that rut?

Go where the life is. If there was a portion of this book that you really resonated with, or found inspiring, or sparked your imagination with all sorts of ideas of what it could look like for you and your students, move toward that energy. It's possible that you were already familiar with that approach to Scripture. You might already be putting it into practice in some significant ways. We often gravitate toward ideas or concepts that aren't completely foreign to us. Start there.

Move toward the content of this book you found most challenging. Eventually, I encourage you to move toward whatever conflict or tension you might be feeling about some of the approaches. Perhaps even run toward them. Maybe the chapter of this book that made you the most uncomfortable or that you had the most disagreement with is the space on the map where you need to make a home for a while. This is, obviously, the more difficult path. However, those feelings of resistance, defensiveness, or disagreement could be coming in response to the invitation that God is most interested in us accepting. Moving toward the place on the map you're least comfortable with and building a temporary home there may not be a recipe for short-term success, but could lead to long-term transformation in your life and in your ministry.

Keep going. Keep growing. Keep expanding the map and inviting others to journey with you.

HOLDING THE TENSIONS

This book is not meant to become a destination, but an important point on the continuing journey of how you read the Bible with students.

Any tension you feel between spaces on the map, any dissonance you feel between chapters of this book, any apparent contradictions or diverging paths forward, may not be problems to solve, but instead a dynamic tension to be held. These apparent challenges in how we read the Bible are a reflection of what the Bible is and isn't.

The Bible is not a twenty-first century history or science book written by God that fell out of the sky with an instruction manual. It's not a system or a formula to solve. There is not just one author or even one single editor behind it.

The Bible was composed by multiple authors from multiple countries in multiple languages across multiple centuries. In North America, we're thousands of miles and years removed from the Bible, not to mention the vast cultural differences that exist between our lives and the Ancient Near East where the Bible was born. The Bible, by its very nature, reflects vast diversity and complexity. To suggest that there is only one simple way to read it is to risk killing its meaning. Instead, we have to be willing to allow our preconceived ideas, opinions, and worldviews to die at its feet.

Let's let the Bible be what it is, and let's be adventurous in how we read it.

BACK TO CHURCH

After more meetings, time, and deliberation, the leadership of our church eventually made a decision about the difficult issue that sparked so much debate. Many people in our church celebrated the decision and the future of our community. Others protested, called for staff and elder resignations, and some ultimately left our community. It was a tense and divisive season.

The people who disagreed with the decision weren't the only people who left.

A number of young people who found themselves on both sides of the issue left our church.

Some of my friends who were with me the evening of that contentious meeting never came back.

I don't think my church's failure centered on the nature of the conversation or the disagreement and division that ensued. I think my church's failure was ultimately that we missed a beautiful opportunity to give our young people an expanding imagination for ways to read the Bible.

My peers saw the adults in our community arguing about what the Bible says in a way that demonstrated to them that they weren't taking the words of Jesus very seriously. The *what* was more important to these people than the *how*. Worse, they witnessed narrow perspectives and practices coming into conflict in ways that squelched a compelling invitation for engaging the Bible for themselves.

We didn't help our young people see the diversity of the Body of Christ and the possibilities open to us by naming different locations on the map reflected within our community. At best, some of our young people felt like they needed to leave the church to find what they were looking for elsewhere. At worst, after seeing this way of reading the Bible on display, some of our young people were no longer interested in looking at all.

But we can show our students a better way.

What might it look like for a community of adults and students to step out of their comfort zones and courageously engage the Bible in ways that we've never before considered?

What might it look like for a community of adults and students to resist a static and minimalistic approach to Scripture, and instead embrace dynamic and expansive perspectives on how we can read the Bible together?

What might this look like in your life?

What might this look like in the lives of our students?

How we read the Bible matters. Let's journey together to keep learning from new places on the map.

FURTHER READING

Bartholomew, Craig, and Michael Goheen. *The True Story of the Whole World: Finding Your Place in the Biblical Drama*. Grand Rapids: Faith Alive Christian Resources, 2009.

Bell, Rob. *What is the Bible? How an Ancient Library of Poems, Letters, and Stories Can Transform the Way You Think and Feel About Everything.* San Francisco: HarperOne, 2017.

Clark, Chap. *Hurt 2.0: Inside the World of Today's Teenagers*. Grand Rapids: Baker Academic, 2011.

Crossan, John Dominic. *God and Empire: Jesus Against Rome, Then and Now.* New York: Harper Collins, 2007.

Crossan, John Dominic and Jonathan L. Reed. *Excavating Jesus: Beneath the Stones, Behind the Texts.* New York: Harper Collins, 2001.

Dean, Kenda Creasy. *Almost Christian: What the Faith of Our Teenagers is Telling the American Church.* New York: Oxford University Press, 2010.

Dobson, Kent. *NIV First-Century Study Bible: Explore Scripture in Its Jewish and Early Christian Context.* Grand Rapids: Zondervan, 2014.

Enns, Peter. *The Bible Tells Me So: Why Defending Scripture Has Made Us Unable to Read It.* San Francisco: HarperOne, 2014.

Evans, Rachel Held. *Inspired: Slaying Giants, Walking on Water, and Loving the Bible Again.* Nashville: Nelson Books 2018.

Feiler, Bruce. *Walking the Bible: A Journey by Land through the Five Books of Moses.* New York: William Morrow, 2001.

Flusser, David. *Judaism and the Origins of Christianity.* Jerusalem: Hebrew University Magnes Press, 1998.

Flusser, David and R. Steven Notley. *Jesus.* Jerusalem: Hebrew University Magnes Press, 1997.

Fowler, James W. *Stages of Faith: The Psychology of Human Development and the Quest for Meaning.* New York: HarperOne, 1981.

Frankel, Ellen. *Five Books of Miriam: A Woman's Commentary on the Torah.* New York: G.P. Putnam's Sons Publishers, 1996.

Gonzáles, Justo. *Santa Biblia: The Bible through Hispanic Eyes.* Nashville: Abingdon Press, 1996.

Harper, Lisa Sharon. *The Very Good Gospel: How Everything Wrong Can Be Made Right.* Colorado Springs: Waterbrook Press, 2016.

Heschel, Abraham Joshua. *God in Search of Man: A Philosophy of Judaism.* New York: Farrar, Straus, and Giroux, 1955.

Heschel, Abraham Joshua. *The Prophets.* New York: Harper & Row Publishers, 1962.

Holtz, Barry W. *Back to the Sources: Reading the Classic Jewish Texts.* New York: Simon & Schuster Paperbacks, 1984.

King, Philip J. and Lawrence E. Stager. *Life in Biblical Israel.* Louisville: Westminster John Knox Press, 2001.

Kugel, James L. *The Bible As It Was.* Cambridge, Massachusetts: Belknap Press, 1997.

Levine, Amy-Jill and Marc Zvi Brettler. *The Jewish Annotated New Testament.* New York: Oxford University Press, 2011.

McKnight, Scot. *The Blue Parakeet: Rethinking How You Read the Bible.* Grand Rapids: Zondervan, 2008.

Monson, James M. *Regions on the Run: Introductory Map Studies in the Land of the Bible.* Marion, Ohio: Biblical Backgrounds, Inc., 1998.

Novelli, Michael. *Shaped by the Story: Helping Students Encounter God in a New Way.* Grand Rapids: Zondervan, 2008.

Powell, Kara, Brad M. Griffin, and Cheryl Crawford, *Sticky Faith Youth Worker Edition: Practical Ideas to Nurture Long-Term Faith in Teenagers.* Grand Rapids: Zondervan, 2011.

Powell, Kara, Jake Mulder, and Brad Griffin. *Growing Young: 6 Essential Strategies to Help Young People Discover and Love Your Church.* Grand Rapids: Baker Books, 2016.

Rainey, Anson F. and R. Steven Notley. *The Sacred Bridge: Carta's Atlas of the Biblical World (Second Emended & Enhanced Edition)*. Jerusalem: Carta Jerusalem, 2014.

Rohr, Richard. *Everything Belongs: The Gift of Contemplative Prayer*. New York: The Crossroad Publishing Company, 2003.

Root, Andrew. *Unpacking Scripture in Youth Ministry (A Theological Journey through Youth Ministry)*. Grand Rapids: Zondervan, 2013.

Rousseau, John J. and Rami Arav. *Jesus and His World: An Archaeological and Cultural Dictionary*. Minneapolis: Fortress Press, 1995.

Smith, Christian. *The Bible Made Impossible: Why Biblicism Is Not a Truly Evangelical Reading of Scripture*. Grand Rapids: Brazos Press, 2012.

Telushkin, Joseph. *Biblical Literacy: The Most Important People, Events, and Ideas of the Hebrew Bible*. New York: William Morrow, 2002.

Willard, Dallas. *The Divine Conspiracy: Rediscovering Our Hidden Life in God*. New York: Harper Collins, 1998.

Wilson, Marvin R. *Our Father Abraham: Jewish Roots of the Christian Faith*. Grand Rapids: Wm. B. Eerdmans Publishing Company, 1989.

Wimberly, Anne Streaty. *Soul Stories: African American Christian Education (Revised Edition)*. Nashville: Abingdon Press, 2005.

Wright, NT. *Scripture and the Authority of God: How to Read the Bible Today.* San Francisco: HarperOne, 2013.

Wright, Paul H. Holman. *Quick Source Guide: Atlas of Bible Lands.* Nashville: Holman Bible Publishers, 2002.

Young, Brad. *Jesus the Jewish Theologian.* Grand Rapids: Baker Academic, 1995.

Young, Brad. *Meet the Rabbis: Rabbinic Thought and the Teachings of Jesus.* Grand Rapids: Baker Academic, 2007.

SERIES AND ONLINE SOURCES:

Bible Commentaries by the Jewish Publication Society (JPS), especially Genesis, Exodus, Leviticus, Numbers, and Deuteronomy

The Bible For Everyone commentary series by John Goldingay and NT Wright

The work of Ray Vander Laan and That The World May Know Ministries

The Divine Hours series compiled by the late Phyllis Tickle is a great guide for getting started with praying Scripture.

For reading the Bible as a book, check out the *Immerse Bible* from the Institute for Bible Reading and Tyndale Publishing. Find out more at immersebible.com.

ACKNOWLEDGMENTS

I'm incredibly grateful for the opportunity to partner with the FYI team over the past nine years, and for the relentless support I've received from Steve Argue and Kara Powell. I can't imagine who I would be without all that I've learned from you along the way.

This project would never have been completed without the love and support of my wife, Stephanie, the imagination and creativity of Matthew Schuler, the patience and persistence of Brad Griffin, and the friendship and encouragement of Josh Bishop. Thank you for pushing me and believing in me.

Many thanks to those who read early drafts of this book and offered vital and critical feedback, specifically Jennifer Guerra Aldana, Stefany Bremer, Zoe Caulder, Steven Johnson, Yulee Lee, Jeremy Morelock, and Giovanny Panginda. You made this resource better. Thank you!

Lastly, I'm so grateful for my former colleagues on the MHS team and all of the Anthem volunteers, students, and parents with whom I had the privilege of serving. We were part of something special together. You all taught me more than you will ever know.

You have
hard questions.

Go ahead and ask.

CAN I ASK THAT?

HARD QUESTIONS ABOUT GOD & FAITH

Volume 1 + 2

Fuller Youth Institute

stickyfaith

fulleryouthinstitute.org/askthat

**FOR MORE INFORMATION AND
RESOURCES VISIT:**

fulleryouthinstitute.org/HowWeRead